A NEW WORLD IN OUR HEARTS

Eight Years of Writings from the Love and Rage
Revolutionary Anarchist Federation

EDITED BY ROY SAN FILIPPO

EDINBURGH • LONDON • OAKLAND

A New World in Our Hearts:
Eight Years of Writings from the Love and Rage Revolutionary Anarchist
Federation
Edited by Roy San Filippo

ISBN 1 902593 61 8

AK Press
674-A 23rd Street
Oakland, CA 94612-1163
USA
(510) 208-1700
www.akpress.org
akpress@akpress.org

AK Press
PO Box 12766
Edinburgh, EH8 9YE
Scotland
(0131) 555-5165
www.akuk.com
ak@akedin.demon.uk

The addresses above would be delighted to provide you with the latest complete AK catalog, featuring several thousand anarchist/anti-authoritarian books, pamphlets, zines, audio products, video products, and stylish apparel published & distributed by AK Press. Alternatively, check out our websites for the complete catalog, latest news and updates, events, and secure ordering.

Book & Cover Design by Roy San Filippo
Photo by RR Jones
www.rrjones.com

Table of Contents

Acknowledgements

This book could not have been done without the assistance of a number of people. My thanks go to the collective at AK Press for agreeing to publish this collection. Thanks also goes to Erika Caswell, Leona Benten and Mikhail Gershovich for copy editing assistance and to Joel Olson for his comments and feedback. Particular thanks goes to Matt Capri, the unofficial archivist of Love and Rage, who provided me with an almost complete collection of *Love and Rage* papers and internal documents. The political choices (and mistakes) over which essays to include and which to leave out, were of course, my own. This book is dedicated to the hundreds of activists who participated in the building of Love and Rage over the years.

Introduction
By Roy San Filippo

THIS BOOK CONTAINS A COLLECTION OF writings from the Love and Rage Revolutionary Anarchist Federation, a project that included activists from the United States, Canada, and Mexico. Love and Rage began in 1989 as a loose network committed to producing a revolutionary newspaper and over the years, developed tighter organizational structures and common political work. By 1993 Love and Rage became a membership organization and constituted itself as a federation. I joined Love and Rage in the fall of 1993 and spent three years on the production group of the newspaper. I also served a term on Love and Rage's coordinating committee.

Love and Rage challenged the politics of North American anarchists, particularly in the United States, on issues such as the role of revolutionary organizations and national liberation struggles and was the first primarily white anarchist group to make a serious commitment to fight white supremacy. Love and Rage challenged anarchists to critically reevaluate their own ideas, and in its nearly ten-year existence amassed a significant body of theory and analysis of its own practice in internal discussions and in its newspaper, *Love and Rage*. After the 1999 Battle of Seattle, there was a significant upsurge in anarchist activity and many new anarchist organizations, collectives, newspapers, and gatherings blossomed. Activists began to ask many of the same questions and debated the same issues that Love and Rage had first addressed nearly ten years earlier. Many of these new activists were unaware that these debates had taken place. This book is a first step in preserving the organizational legacy, ideas, debates, and history beyond the political life span of the individual members of Love and Rage. Hopefully, those who weren't participants in Love and Rage can benefit from our experiences.

This is not an attempt to write a comprehensive history of Love and Rage or an attempt to provide a definitive collection of our writings and ideas. I have selected essays that illustrate Love and Rage's unique contributions to revolutionary anarchist thought in North America, as well as some of the key documents pertaining to the split that led to the collapse of the organization in the summer of 1998. This book presumes no prior knowledge of Love and Rage and does not require an understanding of its internal politics. With the exception of the final section, the articles are centered on topical issues relevant to contemporary activists and are not substantively focused on Love and Rage's internal debates. Those unfamiliar with the history of Love and Rage may wish to start by reading "Love and Rage Breaks Up" and "After Winter Must Come Spring" both of which contain short histories of Love and Rage.

Choosing the documents that dealt with the split within Love and Rage was difficult and I doubt that anyone will be completely happy with the set of documents I have chosen. I selected documents that dealt with important theoretical, political, and strategic questions for contemporary activists and documents that placed emphasis on substantive political issues raised during the split. I edited or omitted documents that contained personal attacks. With a few exceptions, documents appear in their entirety; I made minor edits to maintain stylistic consistency throughout the book and in some instances for clarity; I excerpted some lengthy documents.

THE LONG WINTER

A large portion of the essays in this collection come from Love and Rage's twilight. Partly, this is because political crises often produce some of the clearest and most lucid political writings. As organizations begin to falter, harder political lines are drawn and issues that are overlooked in otherwise easier times come to the surface. As a result, clearer and more pointed politics emerge. So it was with Love and Rage. Though there are many lessons to be learned from the ultimate failure of Love and Rage, most importantly, I wanted to dispel some of the mythology surrounding the demise of the organization; it is crucial that activists understand the particular role that anarchist purism and sectarianism within the organization played in its collapse.

The two most widely accepted explanations for the demise of Love and Rage both focus on its alleged Leninism. From its inception, many American anarchists branded Love and Rage as a Leninist organization despite its consistently anti-statist and anti-vanguardist positions. This was because its vision of building a North American anarchist federation was at odds with what most anarchists saw as the proper role and structure of an anarchist organization and because a handful of members of Love and Rage were former members of a Trotskyist organization, the Revolutionary Socialist League (RSL). A corollary of this "enemy within the gates" position argued that the Love and Rage anarchist project was sabotaged from within by a small group of anarchists-turned-Maoists who sought to steer Love and Rage away from anarchism and towards Marxism-Leninism.

I would caution against this easy answer. Anarchists are often quick to point the finger at this or that "authoritarian" tendency for the failures of anarchist movements and struggles, and these arguments continue that poor tradition. Throughout its history, Love and Rage was committed to self-critically engaging the theory and practice of anarchism and consistently sought to apply new ideas and experiences to help build a revolutionary praxis. An article titled "The Historical Failures of Anarchism," written by Chris Day, sparked an internal debate on what were seen by some in Love and Rage to be key historical failures of revolutionary anarchism. A version of this article, renamed "The Revolutionary Anarchist Tradition," was later run in the pages of *Love and Rage*. This article, and the debate that followed, led to the formation of a small factional group within Love and Rage that authored a statement titled "What We Believe" (WWB). The debate that emerged was not about the past failures of anarchism, but about how the organization would develop revolutionary practice in the future. The WWB document, written primarily by the former members of the RSL, ultimately pushed Love and Rage from an organization in deep crisis to disintegration. Although most of the document simply reiterated vague and unobjectionable principles of anarchism, it advocated two highly contentious positions. First, systemic white privilege was dismissed in the document as "petty and apparent" privileges of white workers over workers of color. The analysis of whiteness had long been a contentious issue within the organization and many in Love and Rage had agitated for race traitor politics within the anarchist movement, with some success. Race traitor analysis places central importance on the role of white supremacy and white privilege in undermining class unity and preventing the white working class from participating fully in revolutionary struggles. WWB drew a dividing line on this issue. The authors of the document must have known (or at the very least *should* have known) that they were unlikely to get significant support on this position. Second, WWB advocated that the failures of contemporary anarchist theory could be solved "from within anarchism," a position that was even more controversial than the document's position on race. Love and Rage had long drawn upon a broad range of theoretical traditions—feminism, critical race theory, queer theory, social ecology, and others—to inform its practice. An important aspect of the politics of Love and Rage was its rejection of sacred texts and its commitment to embracing any and all ideas that would be useful in building liberatory movements and struggles. To many in Love and Rage, the WWB position seemed to be a step toward a dogmatic and purist brand of politics that many of us had consciously rejected long ago.

Revolutionary anarchism should be defined by its commitment to building revolutionary movements to crush the state and capitalism and to build a truly free society. The belief that anarchism already has the answers we need or will need is arrogant at best and dangerous sectarianism at worst. Such a view will significantly hinder the capacity for revolutionary anarchism to develop effective theories and practice and risks making it as irrelevant as the Marxist-Leninist groups whose rhetoric and ideas never advanced beyond the 19th century.

The WWB position puts the cart before the horse. Our ideas and political practice must be born from our continual engagement with the complex realities and contradictions of on the ground organizing, not predetermined by the orthodoxies we cling to. If anarchism is to be a viable force in any movements for a free world, we must be committed to self-critically evaluating our own practice and ideas. "Authoritarianism" is a convenient scapegoat for the failures of anarchism, but if we want to draw relevant lessons from the demise of Love and Rage, we should first turn to the anarchist sectarianism that bears a significant share of the responsibility for undermining this project. The failures of the revolutionary groups of the 1960s and 1970s were rooted not only in faulty ideas, but also because their drive to maintain ideological purity prevented them from recognizing the practical failure of those ideas. As anarchists we must be committed, above all else, to fighting for a free society and to building a political culture committed to ruthlessly debating the ideas that guide our actions.

Revolutionary anarchism has been in a theoretical crisis for decades. It is easy to overlook this crisis because of the recent surge of interest in anarchism that has followed Seattle. But a substantive increase in the numbers of people who identify with anarchism does not mean there has been a corresponding forward movement in the development of the politics and theory that inform our practice. Those who wish to make revolutionary anarchism a force in emerging movements must struggle to offer a dynamic set of ideas that will allow us to examine our own praxis instead of blaming authoritarians within and without for our failures. This is a necessary first step if anarchism is to become anything more than a sideshow in emerging struggles. Until then, despite the occasional swallows we might see, we will still be a long way from spring.

ANARCHY

Always More People Than Cops

BY FUTURA DEMIBOLD
LOVE AND RAGE, SPECIAL BROADSHEET EDITION, AUGUST 1996

CLARK STREET, CHICAGO, AUGUST 26, 1968. The smell of tear gas hangs in the air south of Lincoln Park, which the cops have just gassed out. People have scattered, mostly heading toward the central Loop. The air is heavy, still war at 11PM. Down Clark Street, almost deserted, a cop car glides slowly, blue-and-white paint reflecting the street lights. Half a block from me, a loud POP—a brick has hit the windshield. The car jerks to a stop, its doors fly open, then there's a splatter of crashes, white stars blossom in the door panels. The doors slam shut and the car flashes past me, still accelerating as it dwindles. Soon it's gone, Clark Street is quiet, young voices laugh at a distance in the summer air.

"Revolution is a festival of the oppressed," wrote the 19th century historian Jules Michelet. Chicago '68 was indeed a festival, but not the Yippie "Festival of Life" that drew some participants to town. The real festival came in moments like this, when the balance of force turned over and the real balance of power stood revealed: there are always more people than cops. To a young radical of the time, the week's events taught that lesson and many others—about power, politics, and class.

POWER

In front of the Conrad Hilton, downtown Chicago, probably Wednesday, August 28. A kid tosses something at a cop, and he flips and chases the youth through the front line of demonstrators, which immediately shuts behind the cop and begins to close in a circle around him, people screaming, "Kill him! Kill him!" He runs, head ducked low, legs stretching out, back toward the line of his comrades, who reach through the demonstrators and pull him to safety.

After the convention, liberals tagged the events a "police riot" to turn the blame on the cops, away from mayor Richard F. Daley and the Democrats. Though it contains some truth—the cops and national guard bloodied and manhandled thousands during the six days of August 25-30—the "police riot" idea is false for two reasons. First, most times when cops charged the crowds they were acting in a disciplined way, under orders, not "rioting," but carrying out the policy of the state. Second, more important, it was our riot.

Through the week, there were repeated clashes around three flashpoints: Lincoln Park, two miles north of the Loop, where many out-of-towners were camping and gathering and which the cops gassed out on Sunday, Monday, and Tuesday, August 25-27, enforcing an 11PM curfew no one ever heard of before; Grant Park, across Michigan Avenue from the delegates; headquarters at the Hilton, where there were confrontations every day but particularly on Wednesday, August 28; and the south end of the Michigan Avenue lakefront, at 12th Street, the route for several attempted marches to the convention site at the Chicago Amphitheatre, all blocked by the cops.

Probably only a few hundred demonstrators were oriented to street fighting from the start. A larger number were committed to non-violence at any cost. But probably the largest number wanted to mount standard protests, marches, and demonstrations in front of the Hilton (we called it the "Hitler")—but were ready to fight back tactically when stopped, wherever they had the advantage. This situation created Chicago '68—a mass protest that became a mass riot for hours or just minutes at a time, then resolved to protest again, only to become a riot once more.

Nobody planned, this violence (unlike the cop violence). There were mass numbers and mass impetus. For example, on August 28th, cop brutality at a rally in Grant Park led Tom Hayden, of Students for a Democratic Society (SDS) and the anti-war Mobilization Committee (MOBE), to call for a move on its own. Cut off in the park (which is divided by a lagoon) by cops blocking the bridges to the Michigan Avenue side, the crowd rushed north, crossed an undefended bridge, and returned south to the Hilton, also trying to spill up the side streets around it. The cops controlled the perimeter, but not the confrontation scene itself, and at such moments they lost tactical control on a local scale.

Our riots, then, were a mass action, part of a shifting of public emotion. They succeeded when the pre-existing readiness of some people to mix it up was answered by the accumulated rage in the crowds and where the crowds had local superiority because of numbers. They were not a guerilla, affinity group, or "black bloc"-type action.

Politics is about power; revolutionary power is about power in the streets; revolutionary anarchist politics is about popular, mass power in the streets. When street actions have mass backing—as they did in Chicago, among the thousands demonstrating—then they can win local control over the streets. When such actions have large-scale support in a society, this is technically called a revolutionary situation.

On the other hand, the support has to be there: a good leader with tactical sense can smell when it's there and not. The popular support can't be created just by daring actions. So there was a negative side to Chicago's lessons too, which unfortunately trapped some very good radicals.

Just over a year later, in October 1969, the Weatherman faction of the then-divided SDS held the "days of rage" in downtown Chicago. Ignoring the tricky situation that created mass defiance in '68, they believed one could "create two, three, many Chicago's" simply by going into the streets and defying cops without popular support. They believed several such actions, through the power of example, would "build a core of ten to twenty thousand anti-imperialist fighters." (Weatherman manifesto, quoted in Todd Gitlin, The Sixties, pg. 392)

Aside from the fact that their ideology was fully Stalinist-Communist, Weatherman's strategy alienated thousands of people. They barged into high schools to harangue working-class students and ended up jeered at and roughed up by the students. In the "days of rage," 200 activists, without a shred of support, trashed property and fought cops and didn't gain a shred of support from anyone. Weatherman actions appeared to people just as craziness, something no sane person would have anything to do with. The actions isolated Weatherman and helped build, in response, the explicitly liberal "Moratorium" movement—which held a Washington rally of about one million people the month after the "days of rage." As much as anyone besides Nixon, the FBI and COINTELPRO, Weatherman helped kill the radical anti-war movement.

Politics

Outside the Conrad Hilton, probably Tuesday, August 27. The convention demonstrators have linked up with a caravan from the Southern Christian Leader Conference's Poor People's March on Washington and try to march toward the Amphitheatre, but Michigan Avenue is choked by cops at 12th Street. We end up back in front of the hotel. "Sieg Heil! Sieg Heil!" the front ranks of the crowd keep screaming at the cops. At the same time faces are turned upwards, toward the hotel windows, where delegates can be seen leaning out. Some of the delegates are making V signs for peace, and hundreds of demonstrators here on the street below—the same ones screaming at the cops—hold their hands and heads, making the V sign back to those elusive faces.

The real nature of the Democratic Party seems the hardest of all lessons to learn here. To a minority of demonstrators, including my friends and me, the Democratic Party stands revealed as the enemy, the party of the ruling class, left and right; the "peace candidates," Eugene McCarthy and the late Robert Kennedy, only disguise its real nature. But many more protesters who came here sympathizing with McCarthy or the memory of Kennedy, as well as SDS members and other radicals can't get rid of the idea that the Democratic Party really belongs to us, that it is the party of the underprivileged or should be or can be—if not its mainstream wing, than its liberal wing. And so they flash the V sign to the windows.

For a while, it seems as if Chicago has taught the lesson. "At the end of the week," Todd Gitlin writes later, "the McCarthy people had spilled out into the streets— not because anyone had persuaded them to be anti-imperialist, but because the Democrats' door had been slammed in their faces." (*The Sixties*, pg. 264) But people haven't learned that Kennedy-McCarthy are part of the ruling-class political process; when protest goes strongly into the streets, the ruling-class liberal party will generate a left wing to win them back.

Cut short in 1968, this process plays itself out over the next few years. In 1972, George McGovern is the Democratic nominee on an out-of-Vietnam platform. Though he loses miserably to Nixon, he serves the purpose of coaxing the anti-war movement back into the Democratic Party. Nixon, himself, pulls out of Vietnam. Overall, the US ruling class is willing to sacrifice Vietnam, a minor interest, to keep control of domestic politics. That's the lesson not learned in Chicago in 1968.

Today, the manifesto for the August "Counter Convention"[to the Democratic Party's National Convention] announces "Active Resistance will turn its back on the electoral circus taking place in Chicago and explore instead our vision of real direct democracy." Unlike the protest organizers in 1968, Active Resistance (AR) recognizes that no wing of the Democratic Party is for the people, but AR also implies that the convention is irrelevant, and that's not true. The convention is not an "electoral circus," it is a decision-making meeting of our enemies.

Though its easy now for radicals to dismiss the Democrats as irrelevant, that's really a sign that struggle is low. The Democrats are a party of the ruling class that, historically, has succeeded in disguising itself as a party of the people. When struggle heats up, people will approach the Democratic Party with the same mix of hate and hope as in 1968. It will be up to the revolutionaries to join in protests and convince the participants that the Democratic Party, as a whole, is the vehicle of our oppressors.

CLASS

52nd Street and Cottage Grove Avenue, on Chicago's South Side, Monday August 26, 1968, about 4:30 AM. A couple of dozen bus drivers, most in their light-blue summer uniforms, gather around the Chicago Transit Authority's Cottage Grove bus barn in the city. CTA is on strike, the strike called for convention week by a mostly-black rank-and-file caucus that organized an inconclusive earlier strike in July. I am there, working as a summer-replacement driver. This first morning, there's a strong initial show of pickets, then when it becomes clear that management won't try to get buses out, the pickets dwindle.

The strike issues needn't be detailed twenty-eight years later. They involve both oppressive working conditions and democratic representation within the union; originally a rank-and-file issue, the strikes became a race issue as the largely Black workforce faced a white, union leadership and most of the minority-white drivers stood aside or backed the leaders.

A young radical brought away in memory the pure blue of the sky on those early summer mornings—a clarity that seemed to stand for the immense power of the working class. I had already sensed that power at the beginning of the first strike, when an older worker stepped up into my bus as I passed the barn midway in my shift to say, "Finish this trip and pull in; we're on strike," and the city's bus traffic halted like that, with quiet spoken words.

Each day during the convention, I am at 52nd and Cottage in the morning and at the convention protests later, if I can get down there. But the two movements remain separate. While the drivers know about the protesters—quietly chuckling over the papers and the TV news, liking the protests and bemused over some of the fighting and rhetoric—the protesters have seemingly never heard of the strike.

On one night they do hear, briefly. The strike meeting that night is at a North Side church, not far from Lincoln Park, and a decision is voted to march to the park to show support for the protesters. But the meeting goes on too long and by the time a few hundred drivers march east on North Avenue toward the park, the demonstrators are marching away from the park toward some other target. The two lines of march actually pass, on opposite sides of the street, while I go to the march captains and explain what is happening. An SDS leader, Nick Eagleson, takes the bullhorn and crisply announces that the strikers have come to show solidarity and we will join them in a common rally. So the students turn round, the two crowds hold an impromptu rally, and we celebrate a moment of unity between the protest movement and the working class.

But in the long run, the separate marches are the right symbol; our movement, as a whole, disdained the working class. One heard that the workers were bought-off, white, prosperous—but nobody talked to the drivers I worked with. Weatherman proclaimed that "the long-range interests of the non-colonial sections of the working class lie with overthrowing imperialism" (Weatherman manifesto)—but this was just a way of justifying their actions in Marxist jargon. Neither Weatherman nor most other factions tried to understand workers, Black or white—or most other Black people—except to harangue them.

After 1968, my friends and I tried for many years to organize a revolutionary wing among Black and white US workers. We were wrong about how possible this would be in our generation—but not in our belief that only such a movement could defeat the state and organize a humane society. In contrast, the majority ideas in the 1960s peace movement—that one could organize a peace-and-social change wing inside the Democratic Party, or make a revolution in the US without a popular base, as an outpost of Third World revolutions—were fundamentally, morally wrong. Today as much as in 1968, the link-up that didn't quite happen on North Avenue that August night has to be created, or there will be no social revolution.

The lessons of August 1968 lie both in what did happen and in what didn't. People went face to face with the state power and, on a local scale, won some victories; people launched a mass protest against the ruling wing of the Democratic Party and understood that the DP are warmongers, oppressors; a group of workers and a mass movement of students and youth were in a struggle at the same time and, briefly, made contact. But people didn't learn street action depends on mass support; they didn't reject the Democratic Party as a whole, and organize others to do so; except for a few, they didn't go on to dedicate their whole lives to building a revolutionary movement in the working class, which would have made the generation of '68 one to be remembered.

An anarchist movement worthy of the name has to learn the lessons of Chicago '68: anarchism is not about alternative politics but about power; power lies in control of public spaces; the contest for public space requires winning people away from the Democratic Party and building a revolutionary movement in and of the working class.

Draft Proposal on the State

LOVE AND RAGE *FEDERATION BULLETIN*, MARCH 1997

WE ARE ENEMIES OF THE STATE. The State—the police, the army, the prisons, the courts, the various governmental bureaucracies, legislative and executive bodies—is the enforcer and regulator of authoritarian rule. These structures provide the means with which to maintain control in a class-divided society and enforce patriarchy, white supremacy, ecological destruction, and other forms of domination. The State is inherently authoritarian. It represents the interests of the rich against the poor. It is run by representatives—self-selected and sharing a similar ideology—ratified by the increasingly diminishing percentage of the population that bothers to vote. The State is not democratic, in the best sense of the word, but elitist. It is a specialized institution standing above the rest of society, alienated from and oppressing most of the population.

The State maintains a monopoly on violence, coercion, and surveillance in the service of the interests of the elite. Whether it is their police shooting down poor people of color in the streets or the more systematic elimination of the Black Panther Party and American Indian Movement in the late 1960s and 1970s, the State will not hesitate to destroy those who dare oppose it.

Despite these obstacles we are anti-statists. Opposing State power is an absolute principle of our revolutionary practice and one of the most defining elements of our anarchism. The repressive apparatus of the State cannot be defeated by obeying its laws. For this reason we believe it is essential to actively meet State repression with organized solidarity and resistance. There is a spectrum of resistance possible within a political context. From our commitment to defending each other against arrest at demonstrations, to providing both legal and political defenses for people brought to trial, to supporting imprisoned revolutionaries, we believe that our commitment to each other is our strongest defense against the power of the State. We demand the release of all political prisoners and prisoners of war, but we also work for the abolition of the prison system.

Because we have grown up in a statist society, it is often difficult to imagine not living in one. One demonstration of the power of the State is the fact that it has so colonized our imaginations as to make itself seem natural, leaving us unable to think of a different way. Yet for the majority of human existence we have lived without the State. Initially peoples lived communally, sharing what they had. Early human communities developed a sexual division of labor, with men going out on hunts and for the most part women gathering and taking care of children. Eventually this division became increasingly rigid, and as hunters competed with hunters of neighboring tribes, male warrior groups emerged. Along with the early rise of patriarchal hierarchies other divisions, such as the old over the young and the hoarding and accumulation of wealth, began to emerge. In time these early stratifications developed into imperial families, complete with their own armies, land, and subjects. These were the precursors of the modern nation-state.

Alongside the development of capitalism arose an entity to serve emerging class rulership in the form of the nation-state. Nation-states were created through the merger of various imperial families, establishing economic units that were geographically cohesive, that shared a common language and culture, and therefore made for a common labor pool and market. The nation-state furnished an ideology of national identity that made it easier to rally people for military adventures their rulers considered profitable. The "common language and culture" of each of these new entities was in no way a natural human community like the early tribes and bands. Rather they were created by brutal conquest such as that of the British over the Irish, Scots, and the Welsh, or the Castilian Spaniards' conquest of the Basques and the Catalans.

The emergence of the nation-state proceeded from the unification of Spain in 1492 until the 19th century when nationalism emerged as a general phenomenon throughout Europe. Every step of the way the builders of modern States encountered resistance. The indigenous peoples of the Americas resisted the European conquest. Captured slaves from Africa resisted and rebelled every step of the way. In Europe, peasants consistently resisted efforts to force them off their land and into the workshops and factories. The English Diggers seized common lands that the nobility had claimed. The distinct cultures that States have sought to incorporate have fought back, as is the case today in the Basque region and in Northern Ireland.

Those running States today, both the ruling classes and their political lackeys, seek to preserve their power. Sometimes to do this they make concessions to strong popular movements that challenge them by engaging in direct action from below. In fact, every major State reform has come in response to the strength and power of grassroots movements. In the United States we can look to the examples of the Reconstruction period in response to slave revolts and the abolitionist movement, or to the civil rights legislation passed in response to the Civil Rights movement. As anarchists, we see State reforms as positive, opening up new space for action. We do not sit back complacently when reforms are won. Historically, winning reforms too often co-opts a movement, as when massive labor strife in the 1930s U.S. was quelled with the legalization of unions. We will not get real freedom as a concession from rulers. We will have to win real freedom for ourselves. We seek a true democracy, where the people run their own lives directly. We do not want a "better" State, or a "smaller" State, as many socialists and even politicians now advocate.

The State is not an instrument of liberation. For this reason we oppose strategies for social change that rely on the power of the State. Whether it is participating in elections, petitioning those in power, or trying to seize State power, we see such strategies as self-defeating. Strategies based on State power either fail to appreciate the need to exercise autonomous power to win demands, set the struggle up for co-optation and sell-out, or give us a new set of rulers.

The Marxist-Leninist strategy of seizing the State to create a "dictatorship of the proletariat" has proven a mockery of social revolution, better resembling the old societies they professed to destroy than the liberatory vision upon which these revolutions were founded. In Russia, for example, the "dictatorship of the proletariat" quickly became the dictatorship of the Bolsheviks, as Soviet prisons filled up with anarchists and other left opponents of the new regime and even as the original cadre were systematically eliminated. The way to the Stateless society is not to seize State power, but to completely destroy the State. Contrary to Marx and Marxists, we do not believe the State will "wither away." No State has ever done this in any real sense, and we do not see this as likely in the future. On the contrary, modern States, aided by newer technologies, have found more effective ways of spying on, killing, and imprisoning their own populations as a means of controlling those segments of society that pose a threat to the existing social order.

In place of the State, we propose the self-organized community. We advocate that local people affected by decisions should be the ones making them. For larger geographic coordination, say at the regional or continental level, local assemblies can confederate, sending accountable and immediately recallable delegates to present the positions of local communities. All policy would be made by the people in a directly democratic fashion, with the administration of that policy carried out by accountable and recallable bodies to serve various functions. Various experts, those who know how to build bridges, for example, or design alternative energy technologies, would inform the decisions of the assemblies. But ultimately it is the people who decide, not the experts. This way of organizing society would be one part of an overall redistribution of wealth and power, which would fundamentally change our relations to each other. Of course this direct, democratic form of self-governance runs the risk of evolving into a new State, alienated from and above the majority of people; thus constant vigilance and flexibility will be required to prevent the emergence of new elites and an alienated administrative apparatus.

Another dangerous institution will be any sort of military organization developed to defend the gains of the revolution and fight those who would seek to destroy our newfound freedoms. A libertarian armed force will need to be created to fight the revolution and preserve its victories. The anarchist ideal is democratic popular militias, an armed people. Yet to be successful this force will require a certain degree of coordination and even levels of centralization and command. The danger here is that this force too could become an institution above society. In these conditions we advocate only as much centralization and discipline as is temporarily necessary to win the revolution and beat back any counter-revolution with as much internal democracy as is possible. How to strike this balance may not be obvious; it will be a matter of political debate and decision by the people.

The State is born of the conquest of other people. The self-governing community is a creation of the people themselves in the process of overthrowing the State. The free society is characterized by the radical decentralization of all kinds of power. Confederal structures do not rule over communities; they are the means by which communities cooperate.

An anarchist society is not one free of conflict. It is a society in which the resolution of such conflicts is not monopolized by an elite. The structures of a free society would not be mystified as "natural" and never-changing. Rather they would be open to constant modifications in light of changing conditions.

Submitted by: Jeanne Baren (#10, VT), Chris Day, Paul O'Bannion, and Jessica (NY Local). This draft is based on Roy San Filippo's original, incorporating much of Wayne Price's suggestions, and Chris Day's original draft from way back.

Dual Power In the Selva Lacandon

BY CHRISTOPHER DAY, SAN CRISTOBAL

LOVE AND RAGE *FEDERATION BULLETIN*, MAY 1998

ON APRIL 10, 1998, SEVENTY-NINE YEARS to the day after the treacherous murder of General Emiliano Zapata, the community of Taniperlas hosted a celebration of the inauguration of the Autonomous Municipality of Ricardo Flores Magón. At 4:00 AM the next morning, roughly nine-hundred soldiers and police invaded Taniperlas, arresting six members of the community, three other Mexicans, and twelve foreigners. They also destroyed the auditorium constructed as a site for democratic assemblies and defaced a beautiful freshly-painted mural.

The raid on Ricardo Flores Magón has focused attention on a little appreciated aspect of the revolution that the Zapatista have been carrying out in the areas in which they have a significant base of popular support: the construction of revolutionary dual power.

In December 1994, the Zapatistas broke through their military encirclement by the Mexican Army and declared the creation of thirty-two "autonomous municipalities": democratically-chosen, independent governments based on popular assemblies that would exist parallel to the "official" municipal governments of Chiapas, which are little more than an extension of the one-party rule of the PRI. Each autonomous municipality included a number of communities and their surrounding territory, and like the "official" municipalities, corresponding roughly with the county structure that exists in the US. The autonomous municipal governments were to take on all the functions of governance, including many that had been largely neglected by the "official" PRI-dominated municipalities: public health, settling land disputes, education and so on.

The seriousness of this challenge to the authority of the Mexican state was made evident by the military offensive launched by the Mexican Army against the Zapatistas in February 1995. The attacks against Ricardo Flores Magón in April 1998 is only further evidence that the government regards these counter-structures as a dangerous example that must be crushed.

In the weeks since the attack on Ricardo Flores Magón, the National Indigenous Congress (CNI) has called for the formation of twenty, new autonomous municipalities in the states of Oaxaca, Veracruz, and Guerrero; the Organization of Purhepecha Nation (ONP) has called for the creation of autonomous regions in the state of Michoacan. The communities that constituted Ricardo Flores Magón have also declared their determination to re-establish their autonomous municipality in spite of its current occupation by military and paramilitary forces.

WHAT IS DUAL POWER?

The experience of the Zapatistas in constructing dual power in Chiapas is rich with lessons for revolutionaries everywhere. Before going any further in discussing the particular experiences of the Zapatistas, it is necessary to say a few things about what dual power is and isn't.

The term "dual power" has been used somewhat indiscriminately to describe anything from the Greensboro, North Carolina Woolworth's sit-in to Cop Watch programs to opening a collectively run bookstore or food cooperative to the creation of workers councils (or soviets) during the Russian Revolution. While there is a thread that can be said to run through these various experiences, the unqualified use of the term "dual power" to describe such different phenomena robs the term of any precise meaning. At the same time, it is important to see the connection between these different phenomena if we are to understand the process by which genuine revolutionary dual power can be built.

A situation of dual power can be said to characterize all genuine revolutionary social situations. The classic definition of dual power is found in Lenin's brief article on the subject written in the wake of the February Revolution in Russia, but the phenomena itself has appeared repeatedly in different guises at least as far back as medieval European peasant revolts. In the broadest sense of the term, dual power refers to situations in which a) parallel structures of governance have been created that exist side-by-side with old official state structures and that b) these alternative structures compete with the state structures for power and for the allegiance of the people and that c) the old state is unable to crush these alternative structures, at least for a period of time.

Two qualifying comments should be made here. The first is to distinguish on the one hand between institutions of dual power that have revolutionary aims or are at least perceived as having revolutionary potential (that is to say, they might potentially replace the existing state and constitute themselves as the governing structure of a new reorganized society), and on the other hand, institutions like the Catholic Church or the Mafia that, while retaining a certain autonomy from the state, do not seek to displace it.

The second distinction that needs to be made is between genuinely democratic institutions of dual power in which the masses have real power and more artificial ones in which the formal appearances mask the effective domination of a new emerging elite. This second distinction is not as tidy as some people like to suggest, as there exists a continuum between the two, and a given expression of dual power is likely to move in one direction or another along that continuum in response to developments in the struggle for power. Existing structures that had previously shown relatively little democratic vitality can, under revolutionary conditions, sometimes be infused with more democratic content by the determined will of the people. Old communal village structures have repeatedly undergone such transformations in the course of peasant revolutions. Similarly, genuinely democratic structures of dual power, like the soviets in revolutionary Russia, can come under the domination of an anti-democratic minority like the Bolsheviks and be progressively drained of their democratic content. Generally speaking, the historical experience has been that movements away from democracy taken in the name of emergency conditions is not reversed when those conditions change (when internal and external threats to revolution subside).

Finally, there are the supposed structures of dual power that are under the domination of an aspiring elite from the very beginning and that never manifest the kind of open discussion and contention that characterize genuine democracy. Again, it should not be automatically assumed in these cases that these structures don't nonetheless represent some sort of radical break with the old order. In the absence of any previously existing democratic traditions, these sorts of manipulated ersatz popular assemblies may actually constitute a dramatic step forward in the degree of popular participation in governance. They represent a grudging acknowledgement of the power of the people as a legitimate force for the new state. Neither should it be assumed that the rank and file participation in such structures means that the people have been duped. Such a view negates their agency and flattens out what is always a more complicated situation. While consciousness in such situations is always uneven, many participants undoubtedly see these structures as a means to certain specific ends (land reform, expulsion of foreign occupying armies, an end to certain particularly onerous social practices like foot binding, etc.) and have few illusions about the more grandiose promises to storm heaven or turn the world upside down. They are engaged in a sort of realpolitk of the oppressed: knowing their own strength and weaknesses, they throw their lot in with a new gang of bosses to throw out the old in the hopes of extracting certain concessions in the process.

Keeping all these qualifying considerations in mind, it is still possible to talk about a genuinely democratic and revolutionary dual power and to find many examples of it, albeit generally short lived, throughout history. These instances share a number of important features. The first is the primacy of popular and democratic assemblies in which people have the real freedom to speak their minds as the ultimate source of governing authority. Particular responsibilities may be delegated to committees subordinated to the popular assemblies. Others may be delegated upwards through confederal regional and/or national delegate bodies. But the foundation of power is the people themselves meeting in popular assembly. The assemblies might be based in the workplace, the neighborhood or the village. Elected delegates, officials, and leaders are generally immediately recallable and often subject to rotation to prevent their ossification into a new ruling elite.

It must be said that none of the historical experiences of revolutionary dual power have resulted in the establishment of long-term democratic or socialist societies in which the historically oppressed classes genuinely wield power. All have either been crushed by a resurgent old order or ultimately drained of any democratic content by a new revolutionary elite. At the same time, these fleeting experiences still represent the closest humanity has come to realizing the revolutionary vision of a truly free society. Even when these institutions have finally gone down to defeat, many of their gains have been sustained: land reform, legal sexual equality, certain guaranteed social services, etc. are the concessions granted in the process of crushing genuine people's power. The historical experiences of dual power are important to study, not just because they represent a glimpse of the new society, but also because the story of their rise and fall reveals some of the serious obstacles that will confront any attempt at the revolutionary transformation of society.

The autonomous municipalities established by the Zapatistas represent in many respects only the latest chapter in a long history of revolutionary dual power. In this respect they offer a contemporary example from which certain general lessons can be extracted, much as lessons might be taken from the experiences of the workers councils that sprung up across Europe in the wake of the First World War, or during the Spanish Revolution, or the Shanghai Commune during the Chinese Cultural Revolution. At the same time, the Zapatistas represent in important ways a departure from some of the dominant features of revolutionary movements in the 20th century, and as such offer a starting point for discussions of how to avoid the fate of previous dual power experiences. The verdict is not yet in on the Zapatistas. The autonomous municipalities may very well be crushed by the Mexican state. If they succeed and become the germ of socially reorganized Mexico, that does not mean they will not repeat the experiences of becoming hollowed out vehicles for the rule of a new elite. But there are important elements in the politics of the Zapatistas that would seem to guard against this latter fate.

Speculation on the future is a dangerous game, however, so I will confine myself to a discussion of the development of dual power in Chiapas so far. My intention is to describe in fairly general terms how the EZLN was able to move from being a tiny organization of a half-dozen people isolated in the Lacandon Jungle to a mass movement and revolutionary army able to establish an effective dual power, for at least several years, in a fairly large geographical area and directly encompassing as many as 200,000 people.

FROM DUAL POWER TO DUAL CONSCIOUSNESS

Often dual power is discussed in a way that disconnects it from the long years of thankless mass organizing work that precedes it. It is treated as if it springs spontaneously from the people in the revolutionary moment, without respect for the patient nurturance of the forces that make it possible. To avoid this error, I am going to describe the creation of dual power in Chiapas in terms of four distinct phases of development: the development of revolutionary consciousness; direct action; the creation of counter-institutions; and finally, the construction of organs of genuine dual power. These developments do not proceed in a strictly linear fashion. They are often happening simultaneously. But there is a certain logic to ordering them in a chronological fashion. Each phase created important conditions for the success of subsequent phases even if we can see aspects of different phases unfolding simultaneously. There is a dialectical interplay between the subjective and objective conditions that makes the creation of dual power possible. By conceptually breaking-up the process into distinct stages, we can crudely understand how the subjective determination of revolutionaries to carry out certain work becomes an objective condition of the struggle with success of that work: the creation of a coffee-selling cooperative, for example, gives the movement resources it can then direct into taking the struggle to a new level by buying guns. The creation of the cooperative is a subjective undertaking. It transforms the objective conditions under which new subjective tasks are undertaken and in this manner creates new possibilities. All politics, even revolutionary politics, is the art of the possible. What distinguishes revolutionary politics is the commitment to expanding the realm of the possible to include genuine power to the people.

CREATING REVOLUTIONARY CONSCIOUSNESS

When a half-dozen people moved in the Lacandon Jungle and founded the Zapatista National Liberation Army (EZLN) on November 17, 1983, they brought with them a certain consciousness of their own revolutionary mission. They also stepped into an existing world with its own history of social struggles and previous attempts to build a revolutionary movement in Chiapas. The consciousness of the founding nucleus underwent profound changes over the following decade, and the development of the struggles around them and their own growth had an equally profound impact on the consciousness of the indigenous communities that were to be the EZLN's base of support. While the processes of transformation were crucial in the development of what was distinct about Zapatismo, it is also important to understand that the specific revolutionary consciousness of tens of thousands of indigenous people in Chiapas that exploded into our world on January 1, 1994 did not spring into existence spontaneously. It was the determined efforts of a handful of conscious revolutionaries to build a revolutionary organization that crystallized the scattered and contradictory ideas of people about their own resistance into a coherent revolutionary consciousness.

Within the consciousness of oppressed people there is a constant battle between two kinds of consciousness. On the one hand, we have all been socialized by the very institutions that maintain our oppression: family, school, religion, the media, and the economic structures that exploit our labor. These institutions fill us up with their ideology, with the ideas that justify their power over us. At the same time, there is the actual fact of our oppression, our basic human desire to be free and to exercise control over our own lives, and our periodic experiences of individual and collective resistance that give rise to counter-consciousness. This is a constant battle that one can never escape so long as there are oppressive social relationships. In every individual these two kinds of consciousness exist side by side. The balance differs, the degree to which the counter-consciousness is articulated or coherent varies, but the fundamental fact of this dual consciousness is constant.

Counter-consciousness is not necessarily revolutionary in the sense of taking the form of a coherent grasp of the totality of oppression and what must be done to destroy the oppressive order and replace it with a new just and free society. Generally, the counter-consciousness is alloyed with elements of the dominant oppressive ideology. This "contamination" on the level of ideas corresponds with the actual character of peoples' struggles to be free in the real world. Social struggles are rarely pure expressions of the fight between the oppressed and their oppressors. Aspiring elites and middle forces offer their organizational skills and resources to the oppressed in the conscious or unconscious hope of riding the struggle to power. The oppressed accept this alliance, perhaps grudgingly, in the hopes of improving their lot but usually swallow some of the ideology of their allies in the process.

To speak of revolutionary consciousness then, involves an understanding that is not necessarily something pure. Revolutionary consciousness refers to the point at which the counter-consciousness of the oppressed becomes articulated as a coherent critique of the existing society and a plan to transform it through the revolutionary actions of the oppressed.

The Zapatismo of the EZLN is, in Subcommandante Marco's words, "a provocative cocktail" of Guevarism, Maoism, longstanding traditions of indigenous resistance, and the legacy of the Mexican Revolution (with the decidedly libertarian tinge of Zapata and Magón). The founding nucleus of the EZLN were members of an older guerilla organization, the Forces of National Liberation (FLN), that was heavily influenced by the example of the Cuban Revolution. The indigenous cadre that they were able to attract had received their political training in the Maoist-led campesino organizations like the Rural Association of Collective Interests (ARIC) established in Chiapas in the 1970s by the brigadistas of the Peoples Power/Proletarian Line (PP/LP)—veterans of Mexico's New Left student movement. The Maoists had been invited down to Chiapas by Bishop Samuel Ruiz and worked side-by-side with the Liberation Theology catechists of the Diocese of San Cristóbal.

All of these "outside" forces operated within the context of the consciousness of the Mayan Indians in their own long history of resistance to conquest and colonization. It was their capacity to seriously integrate that consciousness rooted in the historical experiences of the people that enabled the cadres of the FLN to succeed in completely integrating themselves into the lives of the indigenous communities in a way that the Maoists, and even to a certain extent the Church, couldn't. The Maoists sought to subordinate the indigenous component of the land struggle between the campesinos and the landlords. The Church, while accepting certain indigenous innovations, remained committed to the triumph of an essentially European worldview over the persistent pre-Christian beliefs of the Maya. While these weaknesses help explain why the EZLN was able to sink deep roots and grow, it is important to understand the important ways in which the Church and the Maoists prepared the revolutionary consciousness of the people.

Another important point here is that revolutionary consciousness is collective. Individuals can come to revolutionary conclusions, but it is only when they start to talk to each other about those conclusions and attempt to draw out larger more general truths by looking at all of their experiences and drawing on all of their knowledge that we can talk meaningfully of revolutionary consciousness.

DIRECT ACTION

The creation of a nucleus of people with a revolutionary consciousness was the first stage in the development of dual power in Chiapas. The process of bringing people to that consciousness was, of course, a continuous one. But once a certain critical mass existed, they were able to move to a new level—to begin to put their ideas into practice.

Everybody dreams of punching out their boss, their landlord or a cop. And every so often people actually do it. These largely spontaneous acts of individual resistance are self-limiting because they can never succeed in really striking effectively at the root of the frustration that gives rise to them. But as soon as a group of people begins to come together on the basis of revolutionary consciousness, the question of collective direct action immediately comes to the fore: how do we strike our enemies?

The EZLN did not introduce direct action to the indigenous communities of Chiapas. Those communities had been engaged in ongoing practices of resistance for 500 years. Land occupations had been going on for decades before the FLN appeared in Chiapas. What the EZLN did was couple the practice of direct action with a revolutionary consciousness and develop a revolutionary strategy.

The historical experiences of the indigenous communities with direct action undoubtedly contributed to their receptivity to explicitly revolutionary ideas, but again we should emphasize that the leap to revolutionary consciousness was not a spontaneous one. Direct action of one sort or another had been going on for centuries and there is no reason to believe that it wouldn't have continued if the EZLN hadn't appeared. But as an explicitly revolutionary organization, the EZLN was able to put that historical practice into a strategic context and to fight for an approach that took a longer view of the struggle than just securing this or that piece of land or extracting this or that concession from the power structure.

The relationship between the EZLN and the indigenous communities began as an almost purely practical one. The communities in the Selva (where the Zapatistas first established themselves) were facing a rising tide of state repression and violence on the part of the "Guardias Blancas" organized by the landlords who were seeking to push them off their lands. The EZLN offered to train the communities in the use of firearms and in organization of village defenses. The communities accepted this arrangement and sent their sons and daughters to the EZLN's camps to train with the guerillas. But of course the training they received went beyond the immediate practical considerations of community defense. It also involved political training that enabled the sons and daughters of the community to see their struggle for land in a larger global context. With this new understanding they came to see that a purely defensive approach to their problems was a losing proposition. Behind the white guards were the police and behind the police were the army. If they wanted to win, they needed to be prepared to fight the army and not just the Guardias Blancas. The revolutionary implications of deciding to fight back were always there, but it took a revolutionary organization to draw them out and articulate them in a coherent way that could convince people at the moment they were ready to be convinced.

While the existence of the EZLN was a closely guarded secret under the principle of the "slow accumulation of forces" that the EZLN probably picked up from the Guatemalan guerillas, their cadres were active in the ongoing political struggles of the 1980s. They participated in demonstrations and land occupations. When the Maoist-initiated campesino organization, ARIC, split over whether to focus on building a cooperative bank or carrying out more land occupations, the EZLN cadres went with the more militant faction and participated in the armed defense of occupied lands through this period. They also participated in mass mobilizations, including a March on Mexico City and the famous October 12, 1992 March on San Cristóbal (where the statue of the city founder-conquistador Diego de Mazariegos was toppled while armed Zapatista units waited to defend the march if it was attacked.)

All these forms of direct action gave thousands of people direct experience in political struggle, a sense of their own capacity for independent action, and knowledge that the enemy was not invulnerable. These things are all crucial building blocks in the construction of dual power. Without the experience of their own power in more limited contests, it is impossible for large numbers of people to acquire the confidence necessary to set about building institutions parallel to the exiting power structure.

BUILDING COUNTER-INSTITUTIONS

In the process of moving from revolutionary consciousness to revolutionary dual power, direct action is only part of the equation. Of equal importance is the construction of counter-institutions. Revolutionary consciousness means an understanding of the collective power of the oppressed not only to strike back against their oppressors but also to create a new, non-oppressive social order. Just as direct action prefigures insurrection, the creation of counter-institutions prefigures social reorganization.

When the EZLN established itself in the Selva there was already a broad array of what could be called counter-institutions in Chiapas, in particular, various producer-cooperatives for the transport, processing and sale of agricultural products. Such structures play two distinct but very important roles.

The first is to train their participants in self-organization, organizational process, and putting democratic ideals into practice on the ground. In this sense, the counter-institutions represent pre-figurative forms of the new society. There is nothing automatic or easy about building democratic structure. It is a long, hard fight to overcome the many obstacles, starting with our own socialization that this society puts in the way of such projects. Building such structures in the context of the sort of societal collapse in which revolutions actually take place is even more difficult. Every bit of previous experience becomes extremely valuable in such situations. To the degree that large numbers of people are not prepared for such tasks, these tasks will tend to fall to the minority who have organizational expertise, and in this moment we see the beginning of the new elite. The creation of counter-institutions is one of the most important things we can do to prepare for the construction of genuine revolutionary dual power.

A second function of counter-institutions is to provide a more or less independent economic base for the revolutionary movement. The money that indigenous communities earned by cooperatively selling their produce rather than handing them over to a middle-man, became money that could buy radios, uniforms, guns, trucks, medicines, and whatever else the communities and the EZLN would need to take the struggle to new levels. Of course, not all counter-institutions are profit-making concerns. Many, such as alternative media projects or community centers, consume the movement's resources but broaden the base of support for the movement and thereby give it more access to resources. No revolutionary movement can succeed without establishing some sort of economic basis to support its activities.

Just as there is nothing inherently revolutionary in taking militant direct action, there is nothing inherently revolutionary about building counter-institutions. It should never be imagined that by establishing a collective or a cooperative one is actually breaking out of capitalism. On the contrary, one is in a sense becoming an effective capitalist. Successful counter-institutions that really meet the needs of a community can often be easily integrated into the existing social order, and thereby even become an example of the viability of the system. This reformist potential exists in all "Serve the People" projects. Direct action often seems more revolutionary than building counter-institutions precisely because the latter often attracts people who are still holding on to hopes for reformist solutions or who have careerists aspirations for their own integration into the existing power structure.

The only thing that makes a counter-institution revolutionary is the determination of its organizers to use it to build the revolutionary movement by training new cadres and channeling resources into the struggle. This is what existed with the EZLN. Nonetheless, throughout the entire history of the EZLN there has been a struggle against the reformist logic that arises from such projects, against the thinking of those who confuse the financial success of the coffee cooperative with the financial success of the struggle. This was the character of the struggle that took place in ARIC over what sort of priority to give to building a credit union. Obviously, a coffee cooperative is more likely to succeed if it is channeling all of its profits into modernizing production and processing instead of buying guns for the focos in the jungle.

With all of these cautions in mind, it can not overemphasized how important counter-institutions created by the Zapatistas and the indigenous communities were in preparing them organizationally, ideologically, and materially for the creation of autonomous municipalities.

REVOLUTIONARY DUAL POWER

The creation of the autonomous municipalities was thus the culmination of a prolonged process that involved the development of revolutionary consciousness, first among a small group of people and then more broadly, a consistent practice of direct action, and the construction of counter-institutions. These were necessary preparatory steps for launching the autonomous municipalities, the organs of genuine revolutionary dual power in Chiapas.

A situation of revolutionary dual power is inherently unstable. It can not last forever. Dual power is not an end in itself. Rather, it is a necessary stage in the revolutionary process. The question that is confronted as soon as dual power structures are brought into being is whether or not they will be able to survive. There are two threats to such survival. The first is external: the repressive power of the still-existing state. The second is internal: the process by which the democratic content of such structures are hollowed out by various "emergency measures" advanced consciously or unconsciously by aspiring new elites.

An orientation towards the creation of dual power therefore does not go far enough. Any serious strategy must be able to answer how it intends to stave off both the internal and external threats to the revolutionary gains dual power represents, and then how it proposes to reorganize society once these threats have been effectively defeated.

THE CAPACITY TO FIGHT

The question of how to defeat both the internal and external threats to the organs of revolutionary dual power is intimately tied up with the question of revolutionary military strategy. On the one hand, the necessity of defending the gains of the revolution against external enemies demands the repression of counter-revolutionaries and some degree of military centralization. On the other hand, it is precisely those repressive measures and that military centralization that constitute the internal threat to the democratic character of the revolutionary institutions.

There is no easy way out of this dilemma. The anarchist faith that decentralized military structures like militias are sufficient for defeating the centralized military capacity of the state is naïve. So too is the Leninist faith that establishing a highly centralized party-state is in any way consistent with the genuine democracy that is a precondition for any socialism worthy of the name.

The creation of thirty-eight autonomous municipalities in Chiapas would simply not have been possible without the capacity for highly coordinated military action represented by the EZLN. And if those municipalities are crushed it will in part be a consequence of the military weakness of the EZLN. The attention of the EZLN to the military aspect of the struggle is crucial for understanding their success so far.

The formation of the EZLN was driven by certain lessons drawn from the experiences of the 1960s and 1970s. There were about two-dozen such organizations in those years, and despite different degrees of initial success, they were all effectively crushed or defeated by the end of the 1970s. One of the few groups to even survive, the FLN grasped the fundamental weaknesses of the guerilla groups: their separation from the struggles of people, their excessive faith in power of exemplary action by a small group of people, and their adventurist propensity to strike before they had accumulated the strength to really fight. In this sense they broke with the Guevarist conception of the foco as a small group that through exemplary military action, exposes the vulnerability of the state. The EZLN began as a foco in so far as it was a small and isolated group of people. But the strategy of the EZLN was the opposite of the traditional foco. For ten years they built up an army in secret. They trained with weapons and established an effective military command structure but they acquired no military combat experience. Instead, they sent their cadres into the communities and the campesino organizations to participate in their struggles and recruit new members to their army. They also built up a militia structure based in the villages themselves and composed of those who couldn't or wouldn't go into the mountains to join the army but who were willing to fight in the defense of their villages.

The creation of militias is an important counterbalance against the military centralism of a revolutionary army. It creates a sort of counter-power within the counter-power that can potentially stand up to abuses by any new elite based in the army. At the same time, it is important not to make too much of the autonomy of these militias. Many authoritarian revolutions have militias as one component in an overall military strategy. This was the case in the Chinese and Vietnamese revolutions, but there is little indication in those cases that the militias did anything at all to check the centralizing tendencies of the parties they helped bring to power and to which they were ultimately subordinate. There is no reason to assume that the FLN's conception of the relationship between the militias and the EZLN was all that different from either the Chinese or Vietnamese communists. But the results were clearly different.

The EZLN militias are composed of members of the same communities that also choose the political leadership of the EZLN, the Revolutionary Indigenous Clandestine Committee (CCRI), that commands the army. This reversal of traditional relationship of the community with the revolutionary army short circuits one of the most powerful anti-democratic tendencies that exists in any revolutionary situation: the tendency of the revolutionary armed forces to become a power over and separate from the people.

I would suggest that there were several factors that contributed to the creation of a very different relationship between the communities, the army, and the militias in Chiapas. The first is the legacies of 500 years of community based indigenous resistance and the experience of the Mexican Revolution in which local irregular forces played a very significant role. The second factor was the FLN's modest conception of the EZLN. They argued that the conditions for revolution in Mexico would ripen sooner or later and that their project was to build an effective military capacity that would come to the assistance of such an upsurge. They did not conceive of themselves as leading the upsurge. This could be called their first break with the vanguardism of the Marxist-Leninist tradition from which they came. Another factor was the largely defensive view initially taken by the villages. All of these factors came together in the final months of 1992 and the beginning of 1993, when the communities voted in the popular assemblies to launch the war and when the command of the EZLN was transferred form the FLN to the CCRI, composed of the delegates elected by the communities.

Maoist military strategy has always argued for "putting politics in command," which has meant the subordination of the military structure (in China the People's Liberation Army) to the political structure (the Communist Party). This conception is arguably preferable to the Guevarist conception of the politico-military structure in which the party and the army are effectively fused and the military and political leadership are the same people. But the consequences in practice have been very similar—the creation of the militarized party-state. The FLN's practice stood somewhere between the Guevarist and Maoist model. The decision to build the EZLN as a distinct armed organization under the command of the political organization was a step toward the Maoist model. But the separation between the two structures was in many senses academic. The FLN retained a few skeletal structures in a few cities in Mexico, but what made the organization an on-going concern was that the EZLN and the urban structure were largely devoted to supporting the army in the jungle. The decision to transfer command of the EZLN from the leadership of the FLN to the CCRI broke with all existing models. The revolutionary army was placed under the command not of a political party claiming (by virtue of its program) to represent the interests of the people but of the directly and democratically elected representatives of the communities themselves.

The ability of the EZLN to transfer command to a representative body elected in popular assemblies under clandestine conditions is a reflection of the particular cohesion of the indigenous communities among which the Zapatistas had based themselves. It is questionable whether such a transition could be engineered in a socially atomized, advanced-capitalist society or even in most non-indigenous peasant societies. It is even more doubtful that a military structure as large as the EZLN could be built up in the first place if it attempted to establish that kind of popular accountability from the start. The transfer of command was made possible not only by the capacity of the indigenous communities to keep a secret but also by the fact that they had already been largely won over to the revolutionary struggle. The secret was imperfectly kept as it was, and it seems clear that the by early 1993, if not several years earlier, the Mexican government was aware that a guerilla threat existed in Chiapas even if it didn't grasp its scale.

DUAL POWER AND THE STATE

No serious discussion of dual power can avoid the question of the state. One of the things that attracts many anti-authoritarians, including myself, to the Zapatistas is their declared refusal to take state power. Unfortunately, many anti-authoritarians are willing to leave any further discussion of the state alone and just take the Zapatistas at their word, as if good intentions were all that mattered.

The state is traditionally defined as the monopoly on legitimate violence—as the collection of institutions which are recognized as the final arbiters of social conflict: the police, the army, the courts, the prisons, the legislative bodies, and administrative bureaucracies. But this definition misses the most crucial feature of the state: that it exists as a body over and alienated from the people. What distinguishes the existing society from our vision of a stateless society is not whether the institutions of governance have a monopoly on violence but whether those institutions are genuinely controlled by the people. In fact, if we are able to establish political structures that are genuinely beholden to the will of the people, such structures should have a monopoly of violence. This is not to argue against the importance of creating checks and balances within governing structures or of popular militias as the final expression of the power of the people, but rather to clarify that our vision of the new society is not one of competing armed gangs.

The Zapatistas' declared intention not to seize state power is a recognition that they do not represent the Mexican people as a whole. This is not modesty on their part but rather a reflection of their genuine democratic commitments. They have described their objectives as creating an "antechamber" to the new democratic society, of creating a political space in which different political visions can contend and in which the Mexican people can begin to express their genuine will. Whether the Mexican people will rise to this task remains to be seen.

If the Zapatistas have renounced the pursuit of state power on a national level, the question is a little more complicated in the areas where they have real political power. Zapatista communities have jails. They have responsables charged with enforcing Zapatista laws. They have legislative and administrative bodies. They have militias and they have an army. Does this collection of institutions constitute an embryonic state?

The answer to this question is not a simple one. The Zapatistas have struggled to create genuine organs of popular power on the village and municipal level. But it would be a lie to say that there is no separation between the structures they have created and the people. Looking at the particular expressions of this separation can help us appreciate the difficulties in establishing a genuinely stateless society.

In the first place, support for the establishment of the autonomous municipalities is hardly unanimous. There are many purely Zapatista communities and there are many more in which the Zapatistas constitute a clear majority of the people. But there are also many communities with significant minorities that are politically aligned with the PRI or with some other organization that is hostile to the Zapatistas and to the autonomous municipalities. The boundaries of the autonomous municipalities do not correspond with the boundaries of the official municipalities. This redistricting is in part a response to the profound inequalities built into the official structure. But it is also a sort of revolutionary gerrymandering in response to the political geography of Chiapas. The autonomous municipalities are defined precisely by those areas in which the Zapatistas and their sympathizers can claim to have a majority. There isn't anything necessarily wrong with this, but as the Zapatistas attempt to spread this model further and further, problems necessarily arise. It is one thing to establish an autonomous municipality in areas where 90% of the people support such a move and another thing where only 60% do. And how precisely are the Zapatistas able to determine the degree of support that exists for their project?

Then there is the problem of the army. The EZLN is organized, like any army, in a top-down fashion. This hierarchical organization cannot help but influence decisions made at the community or municipal level. There are undoubtedly questions of security that cannot be discussed fully or in open assemblies on which the communities and municipalities must simply defer to the army. At the very least, the demand of military secrecy means that any detailed information about the EZLN's plans, or even general information like whether the EZLN plans to shoot back or retreat, cannot be shared with the community at large. Based on longstanding relations of trust, the communities have so far chosen to defer to the EZLN on these questions. But in the deference we can find the germ of new oppressive relationships and see the process by which revolutionary leadership becomes a new elite. There is an inherent inequality of power between the army and the rest of the members of the communities and the inequality reproduces itself as an inequality of knowledge and organizational expertise.

If the situation in Mexico turns into one of more direct contestation with the state, that is to say revolutionary war this tendency will only be sharpened. The PRIista minorities in the communities will have to be suppressed in one way or another. Matters like transportation and the distribution of food and medicines, that are currently under the control of civilian structures like autonomous municipalities, will come increasingly under the control of the military structure. These repressive and centralizing actions can only sharpen the separation that exists, at least to a small extent, between the organs of dual power and the people themselves.

So far I've only looked at how the particular logic of the political situation in Chiapas contributes to the instruments of popular power becoming alienated from the people and more state-like. I haven't even touched on the more general problem of declining popular participation in decision making. One of the most consistent features of all historical experiences of dual power is the process of declining participation. In the heat of the revolutionary moment, huge sections of the people are willing to participate in the discussions and decision-making processes of a workers council or an autonomous municipality. But people have different degrees of tolerance for marathon meetings and different degrees of patience with the constant political battles that seem to characterize the life of such bodies. Over time, there is a tendency for people to withdraw from participation, to stop going to meetings, and to get on with other things in their lives that matter to them. This process does not necessarily constitute a conscious withdrawal of support for the structures or processes. And if there is another crisis, many people who dropped out reappear and throw themselves into the discussions and the work with gusto. But this process reveals the existence of a certain inequality and establishes the existence of a more permanently politicized layer of people from which new elites have historically emerged. The minority that keeps the meetings going when nobody else is willing to, becomes the repository of experience and expression of continuity. When the new crisis arrives and people flock back to meetings, the minority has a kind of power that it didn't have when people were drifting away.

The Bolsheviks obtained a political majority in the St. Petersburg soviet as participation in the mass meetings that were the foundation of the soviets was declining. By October 1917, participation was at an all-time low. At the same time, however, the revolution was just taking off in the countryside. The Bolsheviks saw in this situation an opportunity to overthrow the Provisional Government and replace it with a government based on the soviets. But the government that resulted was one in which the soviets became little more than a vehicle for the Bolsheviks. This is not to suggest that the anti-democratic aspects of the Bolsheviks' politics didn't determine their ultimate course but to note how the actual dilemmas of dual power favored their triumph.

A related problem is the more permanent alienation of people from the structures of dual power through the accumulation of repressive acts, injustices, and stupid mistakes. To say that an instrument of popular power is not alienated from the people is not to claim that it has the support of every individual in the community. The town drunk or bully may rightly view the organs of popular power as alienated from himself. The conditions for his full participation, namely the suppression of the obnoxious aspects of his personality, are unacceptable to him. Over time, even a perfectly functioning and all-wise democratic assembly will antagonize, one by one, various members of their community through just acts and decisions that are perceived as unjust by the losing parties. And not all problems have "just" solutions. Where a bridge or a road or a water main gets built will benefit some members of a community to the disadvantage of others. In actual practice, no assembly is completely democratic, perfectly-functioning, or all-wise. The need to make the decisions quickly and with incomplete information will mean that mistakes will sometimes be made, and sometimes those mistakes will alienate people. The more people that are alienated the more likely that mistakes will be made. At what point does one say that the structures have become alienated from the people as a whole and have become in effect a new oppressive state apparatus?

The need for a certain degree of repression and centralization under conditions of war, the ups and downs in popular participation, and the process of incremental alienation inherent in the workings of any decision making body: all of these things add up to a powerful tendency of organs of revolutionary dual power to become the basis for a new state.

So what does this mean? Do we just resign ourselves to the seemingly inevitable and abandon the commitment to a stateless society? I would argue no. The vision of a stateless society is neither an idle dream nor a historical inevitability awaiting the accomplishments of the revolutionary state. It is the only vision consistent with real power to the people. There are no ready-made answers for how to overcome the various obstacles I've touched on above. But we still know that the state is the enemy of human liberation, and the struggle to smash it and replace it with genuine democratic structures of self-governance must remain at the heart of our politics.

Neither can we pretend that the dynamics described here are not real and that with pure hearts or the correct program we can avoid these dilemmas. That position is just as irresponsible and ultimately just as defeatist, for by failing to anticipate the real difficulties, imperfect choices and contradictory tendencies involved in real revolutionary situations, this position ensures that those most committed to anti-statist politics will also be the least prepared to put it into practice. We need to systematically study the experiences of all revolutionary struggles, particularly those of this century, examine the problems they encountered and answer for ourselves how we would have handled those problems, not by trying to stuff them into some pre-existing formula but by really understanding the general and particular conditions they faced. And we must figure out how the lessons of those experiences can be applied here and now.

Nor can some sort of anti-authoritarian purism be allowed to become a justification for not getting our hands dirty in the messy world of real-life struggles. The Zapatistas are fighting in the real world to carve out real liberated space in which the project of a new society can be advanced. They have created genuine organs of dual power and must now fight for their survival. Their experiences so far have much to teach us. Will the Zapatistas in victory be able to create a stateless, classless society in Mexico? I doubt it, and that is why I will not condemn them if they settle for something less. They appear to have absorbed some of the right lessons from the failures of all revolutionary tendencies over the course of the 20th century and for this I have some faith that they may be able to take things a few steps closer, which is better than anything else I see around.

CONCLUSION

An orientation towards dual power must be at the heart of any strategy for revolution. But dual power is not something that springs up spontaneously in a revolutionary situation. It is something that requires years or decades of patient preparation. And dual power is not an end in itself. It is a means to an end, a phase in the revolutionary process that precedes the total reorganization of society. An orientation towards dual power cannot negate the powerful stratifying tendencies that will exist in any real revolutionary situation. These tendencies are not simply expressions of authoritarian ideologies (though they are that as well) but of deeply rooted social relations that cannot be smashed overnight and that have their own logic. We have immense powers to remake society, but we are limited by the materials we have at hand. The Zapatistas are currently engaged in the most vital experiment in revolutionary dual power in at least a generation, and will hopefully give us a fuller appreciation of what it will mean to make revolution in the next century.

Some Thoughts About Anti-Authoritarianism

BY MATT BLACK

LOVE AND RAGE *FEDERATION BULLETIN*, MAY 1998

THE SPLIT WITHIN LOVE AND RAGE has been frustrating for me because I think that a lot of the discussion has failed to identify the key issues. In part, I think this comes from problems within the various political theories at work. In part, I think that it comes from our having to come to obvious conclusions and examine their consequences. Predictably, I think that the most important and glaring omission in the discussion has been a clear definition of anti-authoritarianism. In this document, I will offer a definition and will try to show how that definition clarifies some questions.

PART I: THEORY
THE GENERAL BELIEF OF ANTI-AUTHORITARIANISM

Ever since I became an anarchist, I have felt dissatisfied with the available theoretical basis for my politics. Anarchists set ourselves a difficult task: we need to explain what it is that links together the state, capitalism, patriarchy, racism, and heterosexism and also explain why it is that we're against them.

A simplistic answer would be to say: we are against them because they are all oppression. But this is really like saying that we are against bad things and for good things. No one is for oppression. The question is how you decide what's oppression and what isn't.

It seems to me that anarchists say two general things about these "oppressions": (1) they are all hierarchies—that is, they are all systems that unequally distribute social power and resources; (2) they are illegitimate and should therefore be dismantled. Logically, to say that something is illegitimate is to say that it is not necessary and not justified. That is, there is no reason according to nature, that things must be this way, nor is there any moral or logical reason either.

So, for example, we would not say that inequality of ability between tall and short people in slam-dunking a basketball is illegitimate, since it is inevitable due to nature (the fact that heights vary). Also, most people would agree that it is legitimate to restrict people's freedom in the interests of preventing them from committing murder, since preventing murder is morally legitimate.

Once we make distinctions between hierarchies that are legitimate and those that are not legitimate, there are two obvious consequences: (1) there is no point opposing hierarchies that are necessary or justified since they cannot or should not be changed; (2) hierarchies that are illegitimate should be opposed and changed. For example, if it were really true that people of color had the mental and moral capacity of children and white people had the capacity of adults, there would be no point in arguing for racial equality. It is only because we can reject the justification that we can say that racial inequality is illegitimate. We need to give a reason for our calling inequality illegitimate and that reason can only be that we think that the inequality is neither necessary nor justified.

Now, what distinguishes anti-authoritarianism from narrower positions like anti-racism, anti-sexism, or anti-capitalism, is that anti-authoritarianism opposes all forms of social inequality as illegitimate. That is, anti-authoritarianism should be defined as the belief that all forms of social hierarchy are illegitimate because they are neither necessary nor justified.

THE CONSENT EXCEPTION

As we all know, any form of social organization needs rules. Rules in general are mechanisms for regulating inequality. The rules of baseball limit who may and may not run around the bases at any given time—that is they regulate an unequal distribution of power to run around the diamond. The rules of parliamentary procedure (so dear to everyone's heart in Love and Rage) limit who has the power to speak or vote. A system of rules is a system of inequalities: that is hierarchy.

So we appear to a have contradiction: anti-authoritarians oppose hierarchy on principle, but everyone knows that hierarchy is essential to having social life work at all. The resolution to this dilemma has been to say that hierarchy is illegitimate unless it is voluntary and consensual.

Now, you don't even have to think about this very hard for it to be obvious that the question of consent is very difficult. Did the emancipated slaves consent to stay in the Reconstruction South and work as sharecroppers? There is an endless supply of such questions and they are very hard to answer. My point is not to deny such questions but to point out that they are important precisely because we think there is such a thing as consent. Thus, the definition of hierarchy as legitimate only when consensual—opens up a lot of difficult questions of interpretation and evaluation, but it is not destroyed by those questions.

So to state the revised definition in one sentence: What defines anti-authoritarianism is the belief that all forms of social hierarchy are illegitimate unless they are consensual.

WHY ANTI-AUTHORITARIANISM DOESN'T MAKE SENSE (YET)

As I've tried to show in previous writings, this simple definition of anti-authoritarianism begs one crucial question: How do we know what's legitimate and what isn't? Remember that our assertion that hierarchy is illegitimate rests on two threads: that hierarchy is not necessary due to nature; that hierarchy is not morally or logically justified.

Although it is the more common argument, I think it is pretty clear that the "not necessary due to nature" argument is actually the easy one for two reasons. First, it is subject to empirical testing. Second, it almost always ends up being based upon moral arguments anyway.

For example, an argument that differences in educational achievement between Blacks and whites are due to differences in intelligence and therefore cannot be corrected through social changes can be proven wrong through various kinds of testing and experiments. In fact, it has already been proven wrong many times. And many (most, I would argue) claims that appear to be based on nature—like prohibition on miscegenation—only make sense in moral terms. Even an apparently scientific claim like miscegenation should be prevented because it "pollutes the gene pool" falls apart when someone asks, "So what, who cares if the races mix and pure 'white or Black stock' ceases to exist?" The answer is inevitably moral: that such a thing would be wrong. But if destroying arguments for the natural necessity of hierarchy is the easy part, destroying moral arguments is the hard part.

Imagine this scenario. Three people meet: a pro-apartheid Afrikaner, a member of the Nation of Islam, and an anarchist. The Afrikaner says: The Dutch Reformed Church has said that Black people are morally inferior to white people and should be dominated by whites for their own good. The Nation of Islam person says: Elijah Mohammed, a prophet of God, has said that Black people are morally superior to whites and should view whites as demonic. The anarchist says: No one is morally superior to anyone else, and society should be based on mutual aid and respect, not domination and hatred.

Now consider these two questions: (1) On what basis will you say that any one of them is right? (2) What kind of argument will you put forward to convince the two wrong people that they are wrong, so that they will consent to a particular social order if they hold views that are diametrically opposed to (and suppressed by) that social order?

The argument that I have put forward previously, although in slightly different terms, is that you cannot know moral systems are wrong *in a way that will be useful in convincing their adherents to change their minds.*

This presents a nearly fatal problem for anti-authoritarianism. Our politics only make sense if we can (1) know that all forms of social hierarchy are illegitimate; (2) convince everyone else to consent to a society based on our politics. But the problem I've sketched above seems to pretty clearly show that we cannot really fulfill either. Our ideas about the illegitimacy of non-consensual hierarchy are properly opinions or statements of faith, not knowledge. And we are wholly incapable of constructing arguments to convince people who currently hold opposing viewpoints that they should change their minds—not because we're stupid but because such arguments are logically impossible.

MORAL PLURALISM TO THE RESCUE

To my mind, anti-authoritarianism can only be saved from this paradox of its own ideas through one assertion: That if we don't have moral knowledge, neither does anyone else. That is, if we don't really know what's right and wrong no one else does either. And therefore, although we can't prove that defense of hierarchy is wrong, their advocates can't prove they're right.

Thus, even though we don't have moral knowledge ourselves, we do know that humanity exists in a condition of moral pluralism: There are many competing moral beliefs, but none of them can convincingly defend any particular social organization against a strongly held contrary opinion.

From that starting point, I think it is reasonable to make the following theoretical steps. First, since we have no moral or natural obligations to one another, we are morally free individuals. Second, since we recognize that living in some form of society is to our benefit, we can negotiate a social contract from our initial position of moral equality (this isn't necessarily the obvious thing for us to do, but I do think one could argue that it is the only way to start a society from the original position of isolated individualism). Third, no one starting from a position of equality would rationally accept a social structure based on inequality (since they know they would-n't know whether they would benefit or suffer in the long run). Therefore, we can say that social inequality is illegitimate, since it cannot be shown to be necessary, cannot be justified and could not rationally be the result of consent.

Note: First, this is a fast and dirty argument about very complex ideas, and I have no illusions that it is definitive. Rather, I think that I've shown two things: (1) a paradox within anti-authoritarianism; (2) a possible, coherent solution. This is not a proof, but a suggestion. Second, this is theory not strategy. By "social contract" I do not mean a worldwide town meeting at which everyone agrees and makes nice. Rather, I mean that there needs to be some generally recognized way of people con-senting to form a society (hierarchy), or else we cannot guarantee our principle of rejecting non-consensual hierarchy. "Contract" is the historical way of talking about this, and I think it has some advantages (like the legal implication that it is freely entered into and that the parties are equals). Third, even once we've worked out this part of the argument—which is no mean feat—the question of what a pluralist soci-ety will look like remains to be answered. I think that anarchism and other versions of anti-authoritarianism (Liberalism) offer the most interesting ideas about this, but we shouldn't fool ourselves about how much work remains. Fourth, for those of you who've suffered through my previous writing about this, there are two things you might be interested in. First, one mistake of my previous writing was to focus on the impossibility of proving our beliefs before establishing clearly the role of those beliefs in the first place; I've tried to get the order right this time. Secondly, my previous focus on rights is just an extension of the point of moral pluralism—my argument remains that the idea of rights only makes sense if you have perfect moral knowledge, which I have tried to show is impossible.

PART II: SOME APPLIED ISSUES

I confess that I don't have the heart to systematically respond to the various positions put forward during the debate with Love and Rage over the past few months. Instead, here I offer a few thoughts about issues that have come up and my opinion about the options open to anti-authoritarians. I hope this is helpful.

COERCION AND CONSENT: BUILDING THE ANTECHAMBER OF REVOLUTION

One crucial consequence of this definition of anti-authoritarianism is that it creates the well known dilemma of anti-authoritarian revolution: If we oppose all non-con-sensual hierarchies, that must include any that we might be tempted to set up in try-ing to transform society. This is the source of the anti-authoritarian critique of Marxism: "temporary," non-consensual hierarchies established in the name of libera-tion are as illegitimate as any others; in fact, they may be more dangerous than other hierarchies since they falsely appear to be libratory.

So how do anti-authoritarians try to transform society? I think there are three possible answers: homogeneity, non-consensual hierarchy, and consensual hier-archy. To give this discussion some flesh, I'd like to introduce what people in [the New York local of Love and Rage] have called the "Bensonhurst question": after the revo-lution, will we force white enclaves to desegregate? The obvious dilemma is: if we don't force them to desegregate, what kind of anti-racists are we? If we do force them to desegregate, what kind of anti-authoritarians are we?

The simplistic answer, upheld in countless anarchist 'zines are records, is that after the revolution there will no need for coercion or hierarchy because everyone will just get along and there will be no serious conflict. I think that no one in Love and Rage holds this position explicitly, but I think some of our politics unconsciously incorporate this (like calling in principle for the abolition of prisons). As an aside, it's worth noting that Lenin explicitly upholds this idea in State and Revolution; some other time I'll show why this utopian assumption is incredibly dangerous. At the moment, I'm going to assume that everyone in Love and Rage agrees it is unrealistic. This point of view sees the Bensonhurst question being resolved "automatically" by the stripping away of phony differences based on so-called race.

The non-consensual hierarchy solution basically prioritizes solving the wrong of racism over preserving anti-authoritarianism. There are good-faith arguments to be made about why this might be essential to human liberation, but anti-authoritarians cannot agree with them. (That is, anti-authoritarians, as a matter of principle, believe that any use of non-consensual hierarchy hinders the cause of human liberation. This crucial point also seems to have gone unsaid during the recent debates, although it is centrally important.)

Finally, there is the consensual hierarchy solution. Basically, this prioritizes anti-authoritarianism over solving the problem of racism. I think that this is analogous to the Zapatista claim that they are not trying to impose their particular political values on society, but rather are trying to create "an antechamber to revolution": a political process through which Mexican society can decide its future. For anti-authoritarians, there are two key goals: (1) establishing a process of democratic political decision-making and enforcement within communities; (2) establishing a method of determining what people constitute a single community and what people constitute different communities. Thus, if Bensonhurst consensually constituted a community with other people, and there were a valid democratic vote to desegregate, then yes, Bensonhurst would have to desegregate. But if Bensonhurst did not belong to a larger community, or if it did but that community failed to vote to desegregate, then no, it would not have to desegregate and we should not force it to do so.

The general point I'm trying to make here is that hierarchy and coercion themselves should not be problems for anti-authoritarians. Rather the question is whether hierarchy and coercion are legitimate. On an individual scale, that question is resolved through the issue of consent. On a community or political scale, the question is resolved through deciding who forms a single political community and who forms distinct communities. Without this distinction, we are left to choose between simplistic ideas of utter social homogeneity, or authoritarian ideas about the legitimacy of non-consensual hierarchies.

GOVERNMENT AND ECONOMICS

I have a number of differences with people in Love and Rage about the question of how much of a political structure we will need "after the revolution." But as long as the principle is clear—that any degree of political structure is legitimate provided it is consensual (and doesn't threaten the continued freedom of the society) and illegitimate under any other conditions—then my differences are matters of detail. That is, it isn't the structure or extent of political organization (government) that makes or breaks anti-authoritarianism, it is the political relationship of that structure to the people affected by it.

Similarly with questions of anarchist economics. The simplistic anarchist vision of worker-controlled factories with no political oversight seems to me likely to reproduce market competition among factories. Some degree of political oversight is clearly necessary. The dividing issue is not the amount of oversight but the *political* relationship between workers in the factories and the political structure that exercises control over them.

CONCLUSION

I sincerely hope that these thoughts contribute to the discussion within Love and Rage. I look forward to speaking with people about these questions further, on a personal level.

5

On the Black Bloc

BY ICKIBOB
LOVE AND RAGE *DISCO BULL*, JULY/AUGUST 1992

OF ALL SOCIAL MOVEMENTS, ANARCHISM offers the widest analysis of oppression and ultimately the only ongoing path towards social revolution. We understand that as our movement grows, constant re-evaluation of our strategies and tactics is a necessary part of anarchist theory and action. With the growing discontent among more and more people we, as anarchists, have the opportunity to destabilize the state. To do this we must constantly critically analyze our movement's tactics and strategies. This is especially true after the black bloc fiasco at the April 5th demo in D.C.

The black bloc is an effective organizational structure to increase the presence of street militancy at demonstrations. The black bloc at the anti-Desert Storm march in January of 1991 was moderately successful in this regard. Though there were minor setbacks even then (this being the first North American anarchist bloc assembled) the tactic was effective. The January demo took place in a different context than previous ones—there was more anger and tension and the scene was much more charged. The bloc was tactically more organized with affinity groups that were prepared to be militant. This was not the case on April 5th. The April bloc was neither well organized nor effective. It can be shown that the organizational defects at this bloc are indicative of larger problems within the anarchist movement.

Prior to the demonstration, the call went out through the Love and Rage Network, as well as the larger and more informal anarchist network, that a black bloc was going to be formed. As a movement we suffer from a lack of structure in our networks and the only information relayed was that there would be a bloc. More communication throughout both of the networks, as to what we wished to achieve as an anarchist contingent, was sorely needed. And more analysis of the NOW movement in general and how the anarchist struggle is going to communicate with a wimyn's movement dominated by reformist tendencies is needed if we are to raise the voice of our struggle beyond its present scope.

If we are to advance, we must empower ourselves and each other to take back our lives. Many groups pay lip service to empowerment, from Greenpeace environmentalists to politicians in an election year. As anarchists, however, we understand that empowerment is not having politicians keep promises of better laws—these same laws prevent us from controlling our own lives and our own communities. Among the 850,000 people demonstrating the day of April 5th there was no empowerment—only confusion and disorientation. In our contingent, the wimyns-only bloc was invaded by a man who refused to accept the wimyns' decision about the empowerment they feel from having a wimyn-only space. The black bloc, supposedly a tool to counter disempowering demos, supposedly a tool to organize ourselves, left us participants at the hands of the tyranny of structurelessness. How are we to counter this problem in the future?

Throughout the march, no one seemed to know where we were heading or what we going to do when we got there. At one point, a wimyn was informing the bloc what the persons up front had decided. This was not involvement or empowerment.

A black bloc composed of well-organized affinity groups would not fall prey to such tyranny.

Prior to the demo, communication between affinity groups planning to participate should be extensive. Upon arriving at the pre-arranged meeting place, the affinity groups could size up the situation from their perspective: what do we as an affinity group hope to accomplish and see as the best strategy? Does this day offer us an opportunity to be militant? How many police are in the immediate area?

Before the demo, a meeting of either the general body or of delegates of the affinity groups should have met. The purpose of this is not to decide who was right or wrong or who was politically correct. The sharing of information and ideas about what the day may bring is necessary. These delegates would not be rulers; they do not hold you by contract. The purpose would be to communicate the different viewpoints of the affinity groups and to discuss tactics for the day. Giving to these delegates decision-making power about actions and structure is risky business. However, I was for the most part unaware of other affinity groups' purposes and plans. Tightly knit affinity groups that link up like a chain for common purposes create a force that is not easily stopped by the police. Organized action is effective action.

Aside from the wimyn's caucus, there was little organization of our contingent. And when a man refused to respect the wimyn's decisions for their own space, there was no way of dealing with the issue. "The first declaration of freedom for a slave is in denying the master access to her hut." The "would be masters" among us prey easily upon structurelessness. During the bloc, ideological argument is divisive and is counterproductive to action. Why is it that we stand for such disempowering action among us? Wimyn who declare male-free spaces must be respected as it is seen by these wimyn as vital to their liberation. I for one would have been comfortable seeing the wimyn physically remove him from their area. This was a wimyn's march and men present could at least show solidarity.

Throughout the march, designated couriers of information could have helped the anarchist affinity groups to communicate as the day progressed. When the bloc left the general march, we did so at the expense of security and isolated ourselves. At this point, some of us attacked the anti-wimyn's cemetery. This action needlessly jeopardized our security since we were separated from the protective cloak of the larger demo. Tactically this was very dangerous and we should have realized this. When the police moved in, the weakness of our bloc became painfully obvious.

With well-organized affinity groups, the bloc could have disbanded, avoiding the danger of mass arrest and reorganized at a pre-arranged location. Instead, the police played games with the bloc, chasing it one way and the next as they laughed at our ineffectiveness. A participant remarked, "At the best we look silly, and at worst, useless and disruptive." Do we organize as a black bloc to cater to adventurist notions of street militancy? No, it is a means to empower ourselves during demos—a temporary way to take back our streets and to demonstrate to ourselves and to others that there is a future beyond the confines of this state. If we do not better organize ourselves then we are doomed to failure.

6

The Revolutionary Anarchist Tradition

BY CHRISTOPHER DAY

LOVE AND RAGE, AUGUST/SEPTEMBER 1996

FOR MOST OF THIS CENTURY THE REVOLUTIONARY STRUGGLE for human liberation has stood in the shadow of the Bolshevik victory in the Russian Revolution. The collapse of the Soviet Empire in Eastern Europe, repression of the Chinese democracy movement, and the electoral defeat of the Sandanistas revealed the decay within Marxism as a supposed ideology of human freedom. The ensuing collapse of much of what remained of the Marxist left created an opening for the renewal of the revolutionary project.

Revolutionary anarchism speaks to the fundamental failure of Marxism's authoritarian reliance on the state as an instrument for revolutionizing society. But just as Marxism was being tested by history and found wanting, so too has anarchism failed to deliver real human liberation. Therefore, I believe we must be attentive to the distinct current of revolutionary anarchist practice that has sought to confront these historic failures of anarchism.

It seems that Love and Rage has most often been defined by our disregard for anarchist orthodoxies. This is a good thing. If anarchism is to become a serious revolutionary movement, it must develop a new body of theory and analysis and that will require discarding various cherished anarchist prejudices. The revolutionary anarchism of the future should be a living synthesis of all the useful thinking and great ideas found in the course of the struggle for human freedom.

We are not the first group of anarchists to be frustrated by the deep structural problems of anarchism. In this sense, we are part of what can be called a revolutionary anarchist tradition—a small but vital current within anarchism that has sought to learn lessons from our defeats, struggled to raise anarchist politics above the level of naïve moralism, confronted head-on the contradictions within anarchist thinking, fought for tighter forms of organization, and sought to develop a coherent strategy for actually making anarchist revolution.

This article is an attempt to trace the course of that current through one crucial chapter of anarchist history: the period from the outbreak of the Russian Revolution in 1917 to the defeat of the Spanish Revolution in 1937. It will treat only a handful of individual organizations. This treatment is necessarily superficial, but it has provided me with some guidance through the historical predecessors of contemporary anarchism.

MALATESTA

Errico Malatesta participated in a variety of groups and struggles but his main significance was as an agitator and propagandist. Malatesta didn't so much break with prevailing anarchist thinking as push it as far as it could go without a thorough critical re-examination. For this reason, his writings are a useful indication of how far it is possible to go with classical anarchist thinking and where it is necessary to break new ground.

Malatesta was unabashedly pro-organization and divided the discussion of organization into three parts:

> organization in general as a principle of and condition of social life today and in a
> future society; the organization of the anarchist movement and the organization of
> popular forces and especially the working masses for resistance to government and
> capitalism (Malatesta, *Life and Ideas,* p. 84, Freedom Press, 1984, London).

Malatesta is fundamentally concerned with offering anarchist answers to concrete problems of the day. His writings do not investigate those problems empirically, but explicate the application of anarchist principles under various circumstances. The basic weakness of Malatesta's thinking is its lack of dialectical method. His conclusions are not based on investigation of the actual conditions within society (or within the anarchist movement), and they are not tested against the results of their application. Rather they flow from a set of abstract principles and if they don't coincide with current reality, we are patiently assured, reality will eventually catch-up. The revolutionary upsurges in the wake of World War I exposed, in practice, the limitations of this method. Anarchists participated in many of these upsurges, but the most significant anarchist achievements were in Ukraine.

THE MAKHNOVCHINA

The Ukrainian Revolution is a seriously under-appreciated event in anarchist history. Unlike Spain where over sixty years of anarchist education had shaped the thinking of much of the Spanish peasantry and proletariat, Ukraine did not have a strong, well-organized, anarchist movement when the February 1917 revolution toppled the Russian Czar and opened the whole Russian Empire, including Ukraine, to the pent-up revolutionary forces of peasant and worker discontent.

After seizing power in 1917, the Bolsheviks obtained peace with the German and Austro-Hungarian Empires through the Treaty of Brest-Litovsk, which handed over Ukraine to the imperialists. The relatively small Ukrainian anarchist movement seized the moment and built a revolutionary anarchist army around a nucleus of guerilla partisans commanded by Nestor Makhno. The peasantry was already seizing the land, largely without the help of the anarchists. Makhno's army defended the gains of the peasants and argued for the voluntary collectivization of the land while they fought a guerilla war against the white (counter-revolutionary) army and the armies of Austrian and German imperialism. Only after the Makhnovchina had defeated most of these forces did the Bolshevik Red army join them in a final offensive. After the counterrevolutionaries' final defeat, the Bolsheviks turned around and crushed Makhno's army, re-taking the lands they had given away in the Treaty of Brest-Litovsk.

Makhno didn't let the Bolsheviks off the hook for their crimes but also correctly identified a number of the anarchist movement's weaknesses that made the Bolshevik victory possible. He described the original military organization of the anarchists in Ukraine, the "free battalions":

> It quickly transpired that the organization was powerless to survive internal provoca-
> tions of every sort, given that, without adequate vetting, political or social, it took in
> all volunteers provided that they wanted to take up weapons and fight. This was why

the armed units established by that organization were treacherously delivered to the enemy, a fact that prevented it from seeing through its historical mission in the fight against foreign counter-revolution....

Elsewhere the practical requirements of the struggle induced our movement to establish an operational and organizational Staff to share the oversight of all the fighting units. It is because of this practice that I find myself unable to subscribe to the view that revolutionary anarchists reject the need for such a Staff to oversee the armed revolutionary struggle strategically. I am convinced that any revolutionary anarchist finding himself in the same circumstances as those I encountered in the Ukraine will, of necessity, be impelled to do as we did. If in the course of the coming authentic social revolution, there are anarchists who rebut their organizational principles, then in our movement we will have only empty chatterers or dead-weights, harmful elements who will be rejected in short order. (Nestor Makhno "On Defense of the Revolution," *Struggle Against the State and Other Essays*, AK Press, 1996, San Francisco).

Makhno understood that revolutionary anarchists had to operate in the real world of imperfect circumstances. If anarchist ideas were to mean anything, they had to be applied in the struggles of the day. And if they were inadequate to the tasks of the struggle, then they needed to be modified.

THE PLATFORMISTS

Bolshevik victory in Russia gave their authoritarian politics enormous prestige amongst revolutionary-minded people all around the world. Huge sections of the anarchist movement went over to Bolshevism. And it wasn't necessarily the worst elements that left either. In many cases, the anarchists who remained true to their principles were the most unconcerned with making anarchism relevant to the majority of humanity. Outside of Spain and Latin America, where the mass character of the anarchist movement delayed this development, anarchism was rapidly replaced by Bolshevism. In the face of Bolshevik hegemony, the anarchist movement became increasingly sectarian and oddly resistant to challenges to theoretical orthodoxy.

After defeat at the hands of the Red Army, Makhno and many of his Russian and Ukrainian comrades were forced into exile in Western Europe. There they found the same dogmatism and disorganization the had doomed the anarchists in the Russian Revolution.

Makhno and his comrades in exile sought to apply the political lessons they had drawn from their experience and to create a new kind of revolutionary organization—one capable of the profound organizational tasks involved in carrying a revolution through to victory. Their call for the formation of such an organization was a pamphlet entitled "The Organizational Platform of the Libertarian Communists." Published in 1926, it quickly became an object of controversy within the anarchist movement. Reading its opening paragraphs its is not hard to see why:

It is very significant that, in spite of the strength and incontestably positive character of libertarian ideas, and in spite of the forthrightness and integrity of anarchist positions in facing up to the social revolution, and finally the heroism and innumerable sacrifices borne by the anarchists in the struggle for libertarian communism, the anarchist movement remains weak despite everything, has appeared, very often, in the history of working-class struggles as a small event, an episode, and not an important factor.

This contradiction between the possible and incontestable substance of libertarian ideas, and the miserable state in which the anarchist movement vegetates, has its explanation in a number of causes, of which the most important, the principal, is the absence of organizational principles and practices in the anarchist movement.

The introduction goes on to say:

> (I)t is nevertheless beyond doubt that this disorganization derives from some defects of theory: notably the false interpretation of the principle of individuality in anarchism; this theory being too confused with absence of all responsibility. The lovers of assertions of "self," solely with a view to personal pleasure, obstinately cling to the chaotic state of the anarchist movement, and refer in its defense to the innumerable principles of anarchism and its teachers.

If the Platform's words ring true today, it is only because they were not heeded when they first appeared in print. The Platform had three sections. The first or "General" section was the basic exposition of revolutionary anarchist thinking concerning the process of revolution. The second "Constructive" section elaborated an anarchist program for the reorganization of industry, agriculture, and consumption. This section also addressed the question of how the gains of the revolution would be defended by a revolutionary army. The final "Organizational" section called for the creation of a "General Union of Anarchists" on the basis of four organization principles:

1. Theoretical Unity
2. Tactical Unity or the Collective Method of Action
3. Collective Responsibility
4. Federalism

The Platform was widely attacked within the anarchist movement in terms that would be familiar to those who have followed the controversies around Love and Rage. The Platformists were accused of being crypto-Leninists and of attempting to dominate the whole anarchist movement in their effort to build an effective organization. The Platformists were pushed to the margins of the anarchist movement and their efforts to build an organization failed.

The Platformists obviously overestimated the potential for winning over a majority of anarchists to their position. Given the depth of their criticisms, they should have understood that at least they would be able to attract a minority of the anarchist movement to their position. By tying their project to winning over the majority of anarchists, they doomed it.

The Platformists also failed to develop a coherent analysis of imperialism and the profound influence that its global inequalities would have on the process of world revolution. Consequently, their political program and their understanding of the class struggle reads today as very simplistic. But their critique of the organizational failings of the anarchist movement and call for the measures necessary to correct those failings have lost none of their resonance. Their organizational principles are simple and sensible, but they are a stake through the heart of anti-organizational thinking in anarchism.

Tragically, the Platformists were to have almost no influence on the Spanish anarchist movement. When the Spanish anarchists found themselves in a revolutionary situation, they were considerably better positioned than their Russian and Ukrainian counterparts to give the revolution a libertarian character. But in the end they failed for many of the same reasons. The Spanish Revolution offered the best opportunity for anarchists. The failure of the Spanish anarchists to learn the lessons of the Russian and Ukrainian experiences before it was too late is perhaps the single greatest tragedy in the history of the anarchist movement.

THE FAI

The Iberian Anarchist Federation (FAI) was founded in 1927. It arose in response to the burgeoning revolutionary potential of Spain and some of the contradictions within the Spanish anarchist movement. Up until the formation of the FAI, the main organizational form of the Spanish anarchist movement was the National Confederation of Labor (CNT). The dictatorship of General Primo de Rivera had broken up the CNT. Under these conditions of repression, powerful tendencies towards reformism asserted themselves within the scattered anarchist movement. The FAI brought together the most militant and determined revolutionaries in Spain. The FAI was composed of small affinity groups federated locally, regionally, and nationally (including also Portuguese groups and exile groups in France). When the CNT was reorganized in 1928 the FAI came to exert a dominating influence on its orientation. While the FAI constituted the most revolutionary forces within the anarchist movement, they were not united around any sort of coherent program. Rather, they were united in their opposition to any sort of collaboration with reformist forces.

The organizational principles of the FAI stand in stark contrast to those proposed by the Platformists. There was very little collective responsibility, with the result that the actions of the most irresponsible members set the tone for the whole organization. The FAI was involved in a series of heroic but doomed insurrections. This was in part the consequence of the absence of any mechanism of accountability within the FAI. Any local group with sufficient fervor could take action and drag the whole movement behind it, regardless of the outcome. This was evident in the period of 1932-34, which saw a series of insurrections that filled graveyards and prisons with anarchists. The eventual exhaustion of the insurrectionary impulse in the face of overwhelming repression laid the foundations for the widespread anarchist participation in the February 1936 elections in the hope that the Popular Front would free all the anarchists imprisoned during this period. Here we see how unaccountable ultra-militancy can prepare the ground for reformism.

In opposition to Malatesta, who argued that the unions should be ideologically non-sectarian in order to attract the broadest participation of the working class, the FAI declared itself in favor of explicitly anarchist unions because "working-class unity is not possible." The existence of widespread sympathy for anarchism among the Spanish proletariat and peasantry made it possible to build an explicitly anarchist mass union like the CNT, but the very existence of the FAI pointed to the contradictions involved in such a union.

Malatesta argued that the need to meet the daily needs of the members under the existing system has a conservatizing influence on unions regardless of their origins or assertions of radical aims. The experience of the CNT prior to the founding of the FAI confirmed this position. In effect, the FAI constituted itself as an organization of the most advanced elements that fought for (and won) revolutionary politics within the CNT.

Opponents of the FAI's revolutionary orientation attacked the FAI for dominating the union. The FAI resisted this characterization of their role within the CNT and certainly non-FAI members were often influential, but an honest assessment of the FAI must acknowledge its leadership function within the Spanish anarchist movement.

While the FAI was undeniably composed of many of the most committed revolutionary anarchist figures in Spain, they failed to cohere themselves around a strategy until it was too late. The conferences and plenums of the FAI were dominated by discussions of the most elementary organizational matters. The political resolutions are agonizingly vague and subject to the broadest possible range of interpretations. When a revolutionary situation fell into their hands, they were utterly unprepared for the difficult choices involved.

On July 19, 1936, the CNT carried out a revolutionary general strike in response to a fascist military coup. They were joined to varying degrees by the socialist union (the UGT) and the political parties of the left. In Catalonia, the revolutionary upheaval was so complete and the anarchist predominance within in it so beyond dispute that on July 20, Luis Companys, the president of the semi-autonomous government of Catalonia, summoned the leaders of the CNT and the FAI and offered to resign. The leaders of the CNT and FAI declined, claiming that they did not want to establish an "anarchist and Confederal dictatorship."

In this single moment, we find distilled the historical anarchist abdication of political responsibility. The anarchist movement had no reason to expect to be presented with a better opportunity to reorganize society on libertarian lines than existed on July 20, 1936. While support of the CNT was not universal, they clearly had the allegiance of the majority of the oppressed classes in Catalonia. They had created a situation of dual power with the capitalist state. But dual power is not an end in itself, it is a condition under which an opportunity exists to smash the old power and replace it with a new organization of society. Situations of dual power are inherently unstable. Sooner or later the old power or the new power will smash the other one. The consequence of the CNT and FAI's fear of being party to an "anarchist dictatorship" was that they soon found themselves under a dictatorship of the petty bourgeoisie and the Communist Party and then under Franco.

It was only after the revolutionary moment had passed and the Spanish state was reorganized with the generous assistance of Moscow that the FAI recognized the need to reorganize itself in accordance with its actual role. In July 1937, the FAI reorganized itself with clear standards of membership based on agreement with a common political orientation. The affinity groups were stripped of any "official role in the new FAI organization" and vote by simple majority was introduced to prevent small groups from obstructing the work of the organization as a whole. But the new political statement of the FAI was again hopelessly vague and the organization had been fundamentally compromised by their participation in the Republican government and their treacherous call for a cease-fire during the "May Days" in Barcelona two months earlier.

THE FRIENDS OF DURRUTI

The failure of the FAI to provide revolutionary leadership in spite of the powerful revolutionary aspirations of the Spanish peasants and workers created a political vacuum. One organization that attempted to fill that space was the Friends of Durruti, who took their name from the late anarchist-militia commander, Buenaventura Durruti.

One of the central issues in the Spanish Revolution was the attempt to incorporate the militias into a new regular Republican army. Much of the impetus for this militarization came from the Communist Party, which by virtue of its connections with the Soviet Union, was prepared to dominate the command of such an army. Ultimately, most of the anarchist militias were either incorporated into the new army or broken up by it. One group that resisted militarization were the militias at the Gelsa front. Instead of joining the army, they returned to Barcelona and constituted themselves as the Friends of Durruti.

In May 1937, street fighting broke out between the anarchists and the Communists in response to efforts of the Communists to seize the telephone exchange in Barcelona from the anarchists. The anarchist workers initiated a general strike in defiance of the leadership of the CNT and the FAI. The Friends of Durruti played a pivotal role in the May 1937 events in Barcelona, calling on the anarchist forces to maintain their barricades when the CNT leadership was preaching conciliation with the Communists.

After these events, the Friends of Durruti issued a pamphlet, "Towards a Fresh Revolution," that analyzed the defeat of the Spanish Revolution and put forward proposals for its regeneration. Unlike anarchists today who see the Spanish militias as the model of anarchist military organization, the Friends of Durruti had seen them in action and proposed, in opposition to either the Republican army or an exclusive reliance on the militias, the revolutionary army:

> With regard to the problem of war, we back the idea of the army being under the absolute control of the working class. Officers with their origins in the capitalist regime do not deserve the slightest trust from us. Desertions have been numerous and most of the disasters we have encountered can be laid down to obvious betrayals by officers. As to the army, we want a revolutionary one led exclusively by workers; and should any officer be retained, it must be under the strictest supervision.

The Friends of Durruti also proposed the creation of a Revolutionary Junta to be made up of themselves and other groups that opposed participation in the Republican government. They also took some tentative steps to align themselves with anti-colonial forces in Morocco. As troops stationed in Morocco constituted the base of the fascist uprising, the question of support for Moroccan independence was a crucial one. This tentative anti-imperialism is indicative of the Friends of Durruti's determination to confront the weaknesses of anarchist theory.

CONCLUSION

The Friends of Durruti continued to operate even after the ultimate defeat of the Republic by the fascists, but in the final analysis, their initiative clearly came too late. Like the Makhnovchina before them, they only came to understand the need for a different kind of revolutionary anarchist organization as a result of bitter defeats. Their abortive efforts to create such an organization did not get far enough to offer us much guidance today. What they do provide, however, is a desperately needed example of revolutionary anarchism confronting its errors head-on and creating new forms in response to new conditions.

One simple lesson from the experiences discussed here is that the attempt to build a serious revolutionary anarchist organization will inevitably encounter hostility from many quarters, including many sincere anarchists. Only a minority of the most serious and committed activists can be expected to join such an effort. And only in the context of profound social upheaval will the importance of their extended period of organizational and political preparation become clear. Only in the course of struggling to build such an organization can we hope to collectively confront and overcome the mistakes of the past.

Why the Anarchists Lost the Spanish Revolution
Response to "The Revolutionary Anarchist Tradition"
BY WAYNE PRICE
LOVE AND RAGE, OCTOBER/NOVEMBER 1996

CHRIS DAY'S ARTICLE, "THE REVOLUTIONARY ANARCHIST TRADITION" (*Love and Rage* Vol. 7 No. 4) points to the pro-organizational current in the history of revolutionary anarchism. He notes that there have been anarchists who have advocated greater organizational coherence and serious theoretical and strategic thinking by the anarchist movement. In general, I agree with him (although he rather brushes off Malatesta, the great pro-organizational revolutionary anarchist; a great deal can be learned from Malatesta). This is a much better position than, for example, one calling for the abandonment of anarchism in favor of a new synthesis dominated by Marxism. However, when pushing for more organizational structure and theory, it is possible to go off the rails and end up advocating an authoritarian and dictatorial program. The danger of this appears in Chris's discussion of the failure of the anarchists in the Spanish Revolution/Civil War of 1936-39.

THE SPANISH REVOLUTION

As Chris notes, in 1936 the Spanish armed forces and fascists, led by Franco, attempted to seize power in a well-planned coup. They sought to overthrow the Popular Front government, a coalition administration of bourgeois-liberals and reform-socialists. With almost no help from the Popular Front, the workers organized themselves and threw back the military in two-thirds of Spain. At this time, the anarchists (organized in the FAI) led a union federation (the CNT) with half the working class of Spain and most of the workers in Catalonia—the most industrialized region of Spain—and they had much support among the peasantry. Under anarchist inspiration, workers took over factories and other enterprises and ran them democratically. Peasants voluntarily collectivized their farms. Transportation and communications were run by worker committees. Police were replaced by worker patrols. Much of the armed forces were led by the anarchists.

In spite of this, anarchists eventually lost the struggle against fascism. They were to abandon all their principles, joining the capitalist government (including holding the Ministry of Justice). How did this happen?

As Chris said, a turning point came early in the Civil War. After initially beating the fascists in Catalonia, two anarchist leaders met with the (powerless) president of the regional government. He offered to resign but asked for collaboration instead. Garcia Oliver, one of the anarchists, explained why they chose cooperation with the capitalist state. "The CNT and the FAI decided on collaboration and democracy, renouncing revolutionary totalitarianism which would have led to the strangulation of the revolution by the anarchist and Confederal (CNT) dictatorship…[choosing] between Libertarian Communism, which meant an anarchist dictatorship, and democracy which meant collaboration."

That is, these anarchist leaders saw only two alternatives: (1) The FAI-CNT takes power by itself. But the FAI was a minority even within the CNT; probably most

CNT unionists were not anarchists. There were many other workers and others who did not agree with the full politics of the FAI-CNT. In the country at large, half the working class was organized into the reform socialists union (UGT) and others were not in any union. Therefore, if the FAI overthrew the state and established itself as the ruler, the result would have been a one-party dictatorship. As far as it goes, the logic of this scenario seems correct. (2) Working together with all other anti-fascist forces, including not only the reform socialists but the various capitalist parties and accepting the existing hegemony of the liberal-capitalist state. This started them on a road which led to anarchist ministers in a capitalist government, the defeat of the revolution, and the victory of fascism in Spain (shortly before the start of World War II).

Chris indicates that the anarchists should have taken the first alternative, even though "support for the CNT was not universal." But the anarchists were right on this point: seizure of power for the FAI-CNT would have created "revolutionary totalitarianism [and] anarchist dictatorship."

There was, however, a third alternative. They could have called for the federation of the popular committees and councils (juntas): the factory councils, collectivized peasant villages, soldiers' committees, workers' patrols, etc. Federated together, these could have become an alternate power to the Catalonia government—and, spread nationally, to the Spanish state—a situation of dual power. Such a federal structure could have overthrown the state and carried on revolutionary war against Franco without creating a party-state dictatorship.

This would have been more rather than less democratic than the liberal state. Different political tendencies would have been represented according to how popular they really were among the oppressed. Capitalist parties would have had representation only according to their support among the oppressed. Coalitions (between anarchists and reform socialists) would have been based on the real balances of forces. As the working people became more radicalized, their regional and national representatives would become more revolutionary.

The program of a federation of councils was raised throughout the Spanish Revolution by Leon Trotsky and his few Spanish followers. It is true that Trotsky's advocacy of councils was purely instrumental—as a weapon for overthrowing the existing state, not as a framework for a new society. We know from the Russian Revolution that he was willing to ban non-Bolshevik socialist parties from the soviets (councils) and to turn the soviets into mere tools of the Bolshevik party. But this does not excuse the anarchists from failing to raise the program of a federation of councils as an alternate power.

FRIENDS OF DURRUTI

Chris repeats his error when discussing the Friends of Durruti. This was a regrouping of truly revolutionary anarchists in opposition to the FAI-CNT leadership. Chris summarizes their position: "The Friends of Durruti also proposed the creation of a Revolutionary Junta to be made up of themselves and other groups that opposed participation in the Republican government." That is, he claims that they advocated rule by their organization. Not at all.

Actually, they proposed a national council elected by workers from their mass unions. Their program, "Towards a Fresh Revolution" states: "Establishment of a Revolutionary Junta or National Defense Council…Members of the Revolutionary

Junta will be elected by democratic vote in union organizations." This is similar to the program for workers' and peasants' councils (although not quite as good since it required working through the existing union structures). Of course, they wanted themselves and other of like mind to be elected to the national council, but what they were proposing was a popular democratic structure, not a party-state. Unfortunately, it was too late to save the Spanish Revolution.

LESSONS FOR ANARCHISTS

...Time and again revolutions have thrown up popular councils and similar structures, only to be destroyed by the revolutionary "leaders." Today's radicals are divided between the reform socialists (who believe that "democracy" requires them to support the existing bureaucratic-military states and Western imperialism), and the "revolutionaries" (mostly Maoists, Castroites, or nationalists), who genuinely desire to overthrow the existing states—in order to replace them with totalitarian party-states. They see their respective parties as becoming new states. Anarchism (or anti-authoritarian socialism), for all its many faults, is unique in placing the self-organization of the oppressed at the center of its program—the center of both its ultimate goal and of the means to reach that goal.

In the course of a revolution, a certain amount of centralization and repression (of open counter-revolutionaries) will be necessary, the point of Chris's article. But anti-authoritarians should consciously use just as much centralization and repression as is necessary and should deliberately work to keep the communal organization as decentralized and radically democratic as possible. Exactly how to maintain this balance is a matter of political judgment, but we must have no ambiguity on our opposition to party-states.

ORGANIZATION

Love and Rage in the New World Order
BY CHRISTOPHER DAY
LOVE AND RAGE CONFERENCE PAPER, 1994

INTRODUCTION

LOVE AND RAGE IS AT AN IMPASSE. A little over a year ago in San Diego, we made some important decisions about the nature of the organization. For about five months, we maintained a high level of organization, most notably in confronting mobilizations of the racist right. Our membership grew more dramatically than even the most optimistic of us expected. And yet there is a deep sense in which we are justified in feeling we have made little progress. The organization seems to be in permanent shambles and lacking a clear direction.

This paper is an attempt to give a new and clear direction to Love and Rage. It has two main sections. The first section, "The Fix We're In," is an analysis of Love and Rage as an expression of developments in the world. It is an attempt to locate Love and Rage in the process of global-capitalist restructuring and the rise and fall of social struggles in the late 20th century. The second section, "Getting Organized," is an attempt to draw some conclusions about the sort of strategy we should be pursuing and to make some concrete proposals about how we can put such a strategy into effect.

THE FIX WE'RE IN

The most interesting thing about Love and Rage is that it exists at all. In spite of no coherent strategy, a poverty of theoretical discussion, a perpetual state of financial crisis, a record of persistent failure to follow through on planned projects, and other failures and screw-ups too numerous to mention, the membership of Love and Rage grows as we attract new people more quickly than we drive people away. Why is this? I believe that the answer is simple. Love and Rage is one of the few national organizations (if it can be called that) that represents the radical political aspirations of a new force in this society. It is my hope to identify precisely what that force is in order to suggest where we can go with it.

The capitalist media has devoted a lot of attention these past few years to what is called "Generation X." The image of the typical Generation X member put forward in the media is that of an over-educated and under-ambitious twenty-something white youth, often tattooed and/or pierced: the Slacker. This image has been reproduced so often that it is embarrassing to talk seriously about Generation X. The capitalist media has focused its analysis of Generation X almost exclusively on its cultural expressions, the pose and attitude, and the music—that is, the generational qualities of Generation X. This focus has obscured a deeper reality that deserves more serious attention. The cultural definition of Generation X raises all sorts of problems in understanding what lies beneath this surface. There are lots of people who consider themselves culturally outside Generation X or who have a critique of the outlook of

Generation X, who are nonetheless part of the same deeper phenomenon that "Generation X" has become a codeword for in the capitalist media.

Since the early 1970s, a global process of restructuring capitalism has been taking place. This process of restructuring is a response to a number of major social, political and technological developments. In particular, the decolonization of Africa and Asia, the development of sophisticated information technologies, and the insurgent movements that rose up in the industrial countries in the '60s and '70s have compelled capitalism to dramatically reorganize itself.

After the Second World War, a deal was struck in the United States between the major corporations and the organized labor movement that basically guaranteed a large, privileged section of the working class steady improvements in its standard of living in exchange for social peace and support for US military actions around the world. In terms of consciousness, if not always in terms of their economic position in the overall process of exploitation, the effect of this deal was to de-proletarianize a huge section of the US work force.

That deal was broken in the 1960s when anti-colonial movements around the world and the Black liberation movement in the US inspired millions of relatively privileged white youth to openly oppose and defy the US war against Vietnam. At the same time, the enormous expenditures the US was making to wage the war were undermining US domination of the world economy. The other industrialized countries were becoming more competitive, OPEC forced the industrialized countries to pay more for oil, and certain Third World countries, like Korea and Brazil, began to industrialize.

The global capitalist restructuring that has resulted has had several main features. The most significant is the massive relocation of industrial production from the old imperialist countries to the Third World. Hand-in-hand with this de-industrialization has gone a steady erosion in the standard of living of the US working class, both in the form of lost jobs and wage cuts and in the form of cuts in social programs. While the worst effects of this erosion have been borne by people of color, it is important to note that the erosion has affected the entire working class. Amongst the white working class accustomed to a middle-class standard of living, the brunt of the changes have been borne by their children as they have entered the work force. The story is no doubt a familiar one. With either a high-school diploma or a college degree in hand, the twenty-something child of the $15 an hour industrial or office worker is lucky to get a minimum wage job at McDonalds or doing telemarketing or being a bike messenger.

Young workers have always had to take cruddier jobs at lower pay. What is different this time is that these lower wages are not the first step in a progression of better paying jobs. Rather, they are a dead end; the first in what will probably be a series of low-paying and insecure positions. From the point of view of capital, the logic of this strategy of attacks on younger workers is straightforward; in order to increase profits, it is necessary to cut wages. It is easier to cut the wages of young workers entering the work force, who have little organized power and less sense of entitlement, than it is to cut the wages of older workers. This perspective was quite explicit during the 1980s when companies forced unions to accept two-tier wage structures (one tier for older workers, a lower one for new workers) as part of their contracts. In the new information and services industry, it hasn't even been necessary to renegotiate—the starting point is low wages for unorganized workers.

Large numbers of the children of middle-class families, or working-class families that obtained a middle-class standard of living, are being reproletarianized: they are being forced into a job market in which they must compete for jobs, not just with their neighbors but with workers in Mexico and Malaysia. This is what "Generation X" really represents: reproletarianized white youth. Reproles for short. Most Generation Xers may not be conscious of the shift in their class position that has taken place but there is a generalized understanding that they will be worse off than their parents.

Ashamed as we might be to admit it, Love and Rage in the US and Canada is a Generation X organization. (In Mexico the picture is different, but Love and Rage is just as much an expression of global capitalist restructuring there as here. The continental orientation of Love and Rage is really just a reflection of the new capitalist terrain we are on as reflected in NAFTA.) The US and Canadian membership of Love and Rage is almost exclusively white. The handful of members who are not in their twenties are all people who were attracted to Love and Rage by the activity of its young membership. The vast majority of our members are either from middle-class or relatively privileged working-class families. Only a handful of members are from elite or poor working-class backgrounds. And of course there are all the piercings and tattoos.

It is my position that Love and Rage can only escape its current paralysis by looking at itself no longer as the expression of the whole of oppressed humanity, but rather as the revolutionary organization of a particular section of this society, the reproles, that acts in alliance with other sections of society and their organizations. It may be our purpose to identify the interests of the reproles with those of the rest of humanity, but we should not arrogantly attempt to speak on behalf of the whole of humanity.

REVOLUTIONARY SLACKERS?

The position of the reproles creates conditions that will tend to radicalize them. The deepening realization that the system will not give them the comfortable lives they grew up with is already giving rise to profound frustrations. As conditions get worse, larger numbers of the reproles will become receptive to calls for militant action for radical social change. The question is what kind of action for what kind of vision of social change. The reproles are just as likely (maybe more likely) to be won over to internationalist and anti-authoritarian radicalism. Fascism in the 1920s and 1930s obtained its mass following from middle and working-class youth facing unemployment and other attacks on their standard of living. Fascism is already on the march again in Europe; in North America, the Klan, the Nazis, and the Christian Right are all growing.

If we re-conceive of Love and Rage as a reprole organization, then the main task that confronts us quickly becomes clear. We must seek to win over as large a section of the reproles as possible to a perspective of acting in a revolutionary alliance with other oppressed groups and away from various forms of fascism. The details of how to carry out such a project are what we need to talk about. What is the relative importance of directly fighting the fascists and opposing the racist violence of the state (in the form of police brutality and the mass imprisonment of Black and Latino youth)? How important is international solidarity work in this process? To what degree does the fight for women's liberation or for queer liberation undermine the appeal of fascism? What are the prospects for struggles in the workplace, in communities or on campuses?

Do the Right Thing and Not the White Thing

So far I have talked about Generation X in terms of the changing structure of capitalism and the re-shuffling of class relationships represented by reproletarianization. But this is a white-supremacist society and it is not possible to neatly separate the categories of class and race. The project of winning over the reproles to revolutionary politics means we have to confront the question of whiteness.

The reproles are largely white for a simple reason: it has been almost exclusively white people who have been allowed to escape the proletariat in the first place. The post-World War deal between corporate America and organized labor was built on the foundation of an earlier deal that has fundamentally shaped this society; the deal of whiteness. Whiteness is the separate deal that one section of the working class cut with the ruling class in exchange for their cooperation in enforcing the whole system of exploitation on the (non-white) rest of the working class. The price of the relative comforts enjoyed by much of the white working class after the Second World War was the continuing racial oppression of African Americans and the raining down of napalm on the Vietnamese. The embrace of whiteness is treason to the rest of humanity.

The rise of nazism in Germany in the 1920s can be understood, in part, as the brutality of a thwarted German imperialism turned inward as a result of Germany's exclusion from overseas colonial exploitation after the First World War. Similarly, the rise of fascism today must be understood, at least in part, in terms of the thwarted promises of whiteness. The price of capitalist reorganization is being paid mainly by people of color, and the disparity between the standards of living of white people and people of color continues to grow. But those facts are not felt directly by the white worker who sees simply their own paycheck cut and the rise of a newly visible (but still tiny) Black middle class. From this point of view, the existing system has been insufficiently vigilant in defending the privileges of whiteness, and it is on this basis, explicitly or implicitly, in a white-supremacist society, that the appeal of fascism is made.

Any successful revolutionary appeal to the discontent of the reproles must openly reject whiteness in order to be of any use in alliance with other oppressed groups in society. It must explicitly reject any effort by the white working class to cut separate deals with capitalism.

If we attempt to appeal to the majority of reproles simply on the basis of their immediate economic self-interest we will not be able to effectively compete with the fascists. The ability of white supremacy to deliver a relatively comfortable life is a historical fact that lives in the memory, if not the mortgage, of a huge section of the working-class, white people. As the most privileged section of the international working-class, white American workers occupy an ambiguous and ambivalent position. Simply stated, many still have an awful lot more to lose than their chains. In particular situations, it may prove immediately beneficial for white workers to ally with people of color. But just as often there will exist the possibility of a better, separate deal in exchange for treason to the rest of the class. The project of race treason (as articulated in the pages of *Race Traitor*), of undermining the reliability of skin color as a determinant of loyalty to the system has the long term goal of stripping white people of their privileged status and thereby compelling the mass of white people to take their side by the rest of humanity. Race treason is the negation of whiteness. This is a necessary component of a revolutionary strategy. But this negation must be complemented with a compelling vision of a new and better society. Loyalty to humanity must be bound up with the possibility of a better way of living.

THE NEW WORLD IN OUR HEARTS

The most crucial thing that a revolutionary organization can do is to articulate and popularize a credible vision of a new society that is really worth fighting for. The fascists can promise that by putting Black folks or women or queers "in their place," they can return the young, white worker to the semi-mythical prosperity of the past. To defeat the fascists, we need to convey the possibility of something much better than a $15 an hour job, a house in the suburbs, a car, and a VCR.

The new world we need to project must speak to the actual miseries of alienated life under capitalism. It is an impoverished vision of revolution that holds out no more than a bigger paycheck, more consumer goodies, and control over the production process. We need to layout a comprehensive critique of every aspect of life under capitalism and authority to discuss how we plan to transform it. If the vast majority of people "lead lives of quiet desperation," we need to speak to all the things that add up to that desperation: the loneliness and ugliness of the lives we are always painting a happy face on, the shitty food we eat, the fucked-up sex we have, the compulsions and neuroses that cripple our efforts to be who we want to be, the plastic culture, and the poisoned physical environment we know is wrong but numb ourselves to anyway.

Just as important as building a revolutionary organization is nurturing broader cultures of resistance that embody the vision of a new world we are fighting for. While the focus of this paper is on the building of a revolutionary organization, that project needs to be placed within the larger context of a revolutionary movement and the cultures it emerges from. To succeed, a revolutionary organization will need to identify itself with these cultures in popular consciousness and at the same time retain a critical relationship with them that is rooted in a coherent vision of the transformation of all aspects of daily life.

LET'S TALK ABOUT SEX

Over sixty years ago, Wilheim Reich pleaded with the German Communist Party to understand the role of authoritarian social conditioning in the rise of fascism and the importance of sexual liberation as part of any serious revolutionary politics. Reich's vision of sexual liberation may seem impoverished to us now (he was a male chauvinist and a homophobe), but the essence of his argument is still applicable to our current situation. In short, Reich argued that the fascists could successfully channel mass discontent into a longing for the comfort of authoritarian order so long as the revolutionary movement refused to struggle directly against the processes and institutions (the family, the church, the schools) of authoritarian conditioning.

If we combine a feminist analysis of the role of sexual violence and terror in the patriarchal family with Reich's analysis of the function of sexual repression in creating the personality structures of tyrants and their obedient followers, we can see why

it is important to take on these structures. The women's and queer liberation movements have posed a profound challenge to the authoritarian structure of contemporary society. These movements' demands for basic civil rights can be absorbed by the
existing order. But the corrosive effect on a general respect for authority that they set
in motion by challenging deeply socialized beliefs about the role of women and the
limits of sexuality are a more serious threat. The Christian Right understands this.
Their relentless assault on the queer movement is more than a cynical play to popular prejudices; it reflects a serious estimation on their part of what is the greatest threat
to their vision of society.

The disintegration of family structures is a fact of life in the late 20th century. This constitutes the falling away of one of the last pieces of human community that
many people have. Fascism in general, and the Christian Right in particular, promise
to restore something that probably cannot be restored. But to defeat them, we must
convey the bold possibility of a new kind of human community in which sexual
repression and the oppression of women are not the glue that holds things together....

THE NEW SOCIAL MOVEMENTS

While the typical Love and Rage member may fit the reprole profile, very few (if any)
of us were first radicalized in the course of an economic struggle in which we had a
direct and immediate self-interest. If we have participated in such struggles, it is
because we have made life decisions as a consequence of our radicalism that have
changed our social position (moving into a squat, doing workplace organizing, etc.).
Almost all of us radicalized as a result of our participation in what are frequently called the New Social Movements (feminism, queer liberation, ecology,
anti-militarism, etc.).

The New Social Movements (NSMs) have their roots in the upheavals of the
1960s. The struggles of African Americans and then the Vietnamese raised the possibility of the radical transformation of all aspects of society. In response to this possibility, a wide range of social movements emerged. At first, these movements embraced
the revolutionary spirit of the times and saw themselves, in some way or another, as
acting in alliance with the various other struggles then taking place. On a theoretical
level, these movements challenged the narrow politics of the New Left that saw all
questions through the lens of the struggle against capitalism and imperialism.
Eventually, the revolutionary movement was lost, but the NSMs set in motion by the
events of the '60s did not disappear. Instead, they moved to the center of radical or
oppositional politics in the US. Over the '70s and '80s the NSMs developed more
sophisticated analyses of gender, sexuality, ecology, and so on. But they also lost much
of their original revolutionary spirit and adopted increasingly reformist and
fragmented or single-issue approaches to struggle.

THE RE-EMERGENCE OF ANARCHISM

In the 1980s, the anarchist movement re-emerged in part as an expression of the frustration of many younger activists with the caution and narrowness of the concerns of
the New Social Movements. These younger activists saw in anarchism a theoretical
framework, a utopian spirit, and militant practice that could link up a number of different struggles and lead to a renewal of the revolutionary spirit that had once infused

them. The NSMs developed their own social theories in response to the often-crude class reductionism of the (now old) New Left. But in the process, they often became uncritical of the middle-class domination of their own movements. The new anarchist movement did not at first identify its antagonism with the established organizations of the NSMs as a class antagonism involving its own interests—though it generally embraced a class-based criticism of them.

In retrospect, the development of Love and Rage can be seen as part of a longer (and still embryonic) process of the emergence of a revolutionary reprole consciousness out of the middle-class dominated NSMs (in particular the anti-militarist and ecological struggles of the 1980s). Anarchism, with its rejection of orthodoxy and willingness to embrace a diverse range of struggles, represented the closest thing around to a theory that would meet the needs of the reproles. But anarchism carries a certain amount of historical baggage that, combined with certain habits picked up from the NSMs, has been a hindrance to the development of a strong revolutionary current among the reproles. In Europe, where the historical experience of anarchism has a more prominent place in political consciousness, there is also a deeper awareness of its historical failings and weaknesses. (The European counterparts of the young activists who turned towards anarchism in North America instead tended to embrace the libertarian Marxism of the autonomist currents that emerged first in Italy in the '70s and then established themselves in most of Western and Central Europe.)

ANARCHISM AND THE CRISIS ON THE LEFT

The current stagnation within the anarchist movement (the poverty of theoretical discussion and the absence of any meaningful initiative in the field of action) cannot be separated from the larger crisis of the left. Since the early 1980s, there has been a growing acknowledgement by all but the most dogmatic and sectarian forces that there is a profound crisis on the left. This crisis is reflected in the general failure of the left to effectively generate any sort of mass enthusiasm for its politics and in its ability to adequately explain new developments in the world. A series of blows came in 1989 that precipitated a collapse of much of the already withered organized left. The Tiananmen Square massacre, the collapse of the Soviet Empire in Eastern Europe, and the electoral defeat of the Sandinistas combined to demoralize almost every wing of the radical left.

For a while it was possible for anarchists to define themselves outside this crisis on the left. The anarchist movement had seemingly no investment in the success of either the Leninist or Social Democratic projects. Much of the failure of the left was generally acknowledged to be related to its statism and authoritarianism. We could smugly say, "I told you so."

But anarchism is a part of the left and the crisis on the left affects us as well. Since the defeat of the Spanish revolution in the 1930s, the anarchist movement has been largely marginalized among revolutionary-minded people. The anarchist movement has generally contented itself with the role of perpetual gadfly, always annoying and occasionally pricking the consciences of those in control of real mass movements. The result has been a deep poverty of serious revolutionary anarchist theory, a substitution of moral posture for critical political analysis.

It is not too difficult for us as anarchists to see why the collapse of Stalinist regimes around the world would deeply shake the Trotskyist movement in spite of their protestations that those regimes did not represent their politics. Trotskyism's identity is built around distinguishing itself from Stalinism. With Stalinism "gone," so goes much of what distinguishes Trotskyism from other varieties of Leninism and it stands revealed as arcane scholasticism. While anarchism has an important pre-Leninist history, what it has meant to be an anarchist for the past seventy-five years has been defined around our opposition to Leninism. For most of the past century, the so-called socialist states have had a dominating or hegemonic influence on the thinking of revolutionary minded people. All currents of revolutionary thought, including anarchism, have stood in the shadows of these state ideologies and have had their development stunted as a result.

The question that the current situation asks of the anarchist movement is no longer "How is what you stand for different than what exists in Russia (or Cuba or China)?" but rather, "How do you explain what is happening in the world now?" and "How do you propose to build a new revolutionary movement from the wreckage of the old?" Unfortunately, most of the anarchist movement is not really interested in venturing into such uncharted theoretical territory, preferring the comfort of a stock set of slogans and pat answers to questions that now have entirely different meanings.

In the 1980s, it made a certain sense for a group of young activists who wanted to challenge the orthodoxies of both the NSMs and "the left" to identify themselves as anarchists. The anti-statism, anti-authoritarianism, and visionary utopianism of anarchism must be essential ingredients of any serious new revolutionary movement, and the historic tradition of anarchism gave a certain legitimacy (at least in our own eyes) to our often raw and imprecise politics. (In Europe, where identifying with anarchism carries much more specific historical baggage, like-minded radicals identified themselves as autonomists.)

In the 1990s, I believe, the implications of calling ourselves "anarchists" is different. The identification with a historical tradition at a moment when the totality of left politics (libertarian and authoritarian) is in serious question, puts us not so much in the camp of that particular historical tradition, but in the camp of defenders of *Historical Tradition*. That is to say that calling ourselves "anarchists" identifies us not as anti-authoritarians but as ideological dinosaurs defending a set of politics that are not so much wrong as they are irrelevant. The weight of anarchist history is no longer an anchor holding us steady in the stormy sea of the authoritarian left but a set of concrete boots dragging us to our deaths in the muck at the bottom of a stagnant lake. The question here is neither the importance of history or of proper respect for our anti-authoritarian ancestors. Future generations will still have much to learn from Durruti, Goldman, Makhno, the Magóns, and others. But it is no longer clear to me why this tradition is more important, for example, than those of the Abolitionists, of the Seminoles, of the League of Revolutionary Black Workers. It is clear to me that otherwise critically thinking anarchists, instead of grappling with the new terrain we are on, rely on unexamined anarchist orthodoxies, most notably on questions of organization.

While the left as a whole was KO'ed by the one-two punch of the events of 1989 and the Gulf War in 1991, organizational remnants persist. Different remnants have responded to the new circumstances in one of two ways—either acknowledging the general failure of the left or publicly insisting that nothing has changed and that the current situation calls for the courageous defense of old ideas. Anarchists must make a similar choice between a commitment to rethinking our politics and defending tradition.

It is understandable why, with radical politics in retreat almost everywhere, defending ideas that have informed the struggles of generations might offer comfort in the face of an uncertain future. But comfort is not a revolutionary virtue; we need to face this new situation with the courage to confront the unknown.

GETTING ORGANIZED

The lengthy exploration of the current political situation above is crucial to confronting the organizational problems that confound Love and Rage. It is tempting to ascribe our organizational failings to individual screw-ups or to look for a magic solution in some structural formula. This fails to understand that organizations are expressions of larger social forces. There are particular choices that confront us, and how we respond to them is important. But we make these choices in a context, and what is a good organizational formula in one situation may be political suicide in another. The following discussion is based on the assumption that building a continental revolutionary organization is a crucial task because the existence of such formal structures is necessary if explosive social contradictions are to be transformed into effective movements for change. Building Love and Rage is about preparing for revolution by putting in place a structure that will be of use in a revolutionary situation.

THE STRUGGLE FOR ORGANIZATION

At the 1993 Love and Rage conference in San Diego, a number of people who opposed the decisions that were made there felt that they were unfairly characterized as "anti-organizational." And indeed, since then, most of these people have proceeded to build important local anarchist groups. If the question of organization was a simple one of "for it" or "against it" we would be in much better shape. Building a serious revolutionary organization is not simply a matter of identifying the self-evidently correct structure and then filling it up with members. A revolutionary organization must be built on the basis of a conception of its role in the revolutionary process and the correct direction in which the organization must move. People will leave and new people will join as a result of any important decision we make.

A serious revolutionary organization can only be built through a process of continuous struggle. That struggle must include both the larger social struggles in the outside world and the struggles within the organization over the interpretation of what is taking place in the outside world. It is only through such a process that a revolutionary organization can hope to be politically prepared for a situation in which revolutionary change is a real possibility. Our failure to understand things correctly may cause unnecessary delays or defeats to the revolutionary movement. Differences over the interpretation of what is going on in the world are quite literally matters of life and death and should be treated accordingly.

THE PRIMACY OF POLITICS

There is a tendency in the anarchist movement when talking about questions of organization to become preoccupied with questions of internal dynamics at the expense of talking about what the organization is going to do in the world outside it. This is not to say that internal dynamics are not important. It is to say that the internal dynamics of an organization that doesn't have an impact on the world outside of itself will be consistently lousy, as people who joined the organization in order to change the world are thwarted and feed on each other's inevitable failings.

If Love and Rage is to become an effective revolutionary organization, its development must be driven not by a desire to perfect its internal life, but by an effort to make it useful in the struggle to change the world. Such an effort must be informed by a constant and lively debate about the nature of the world we are trying to change and the events and developments that are taking place within that world. For such a debate to flourish, there needs to be an atmosphere that encourages crucial theoretical work. Theoretical work, the work of studying and discussing questions about the nature of this society and what it will take to transform it, is an absolutely central element of what it means for us to prepare ourselves for a revolutionary situation. We can be the most kick-ass militant and theoretical participants in demonstrations, but without clear and correct ideas guiding our actions this militancy makes little contribution to building a truly revolutionary movement.

2

What Kind of Revolutionary Organization is Useful Today?

LOVE AND RAGE EDITORIAL, MARCH/APRIL 1995

THE MULTIPLE PROBLEMS FACING THE WORLD today require a revolutionary response. The ineffectiveness of liberalism to address the needs and demands of the oppressed, especially of people of color throughout the world, is not due to the promise of liberal democracy being yet unfulfilled but to the inherent contradictions within liberalism and capitalism itself. Because capitalism requires the many to work for the profits of the few, modern society cannot provide full freedom and human liberation for all. The problems of this world cannot be addressed without an expanded and fuller vision of a free society than capitalism can provide. Because capital will not surrender its privileged position without a fight, this struggle for a truly free society requires a revolutionary struggle against capital and all forms of oppression.

Given this, the question is: what kind of revolutionary organization is effective at this time? Historically, there have been two answers to this question. The most common (though not the most popular) has been the vanguard party of Marxism-Leninism. The vanguard strategy from the Russian Revolution to the present is to build an organization of an elite cadre of militants who will guide the masses through a revolution and lead them to a socialist society. This strategy has proven to be an utter failure because it has failed to fulfill the promise of freedom. By creating a highly centralized and undemocratic organization, vanguard strategies for revolution have reproduced these same power structures in society, with the Party as the new ruling class.

The second strategy is much less well known but is currently popular in many North American anarchist circles. This strategy, which could be called the "organic" approach to social change, advocates creating "temporary autonomous zones" (TAZ) of collectives, infoshops, community centers, and other counter-cultural outposts throughout the country to serve as models from which thousands of other "TAZs" will organically spring up from society like a cell replicating itself, changing society without a center or hierarchical chain of command. This strategy is admirable for its critique of all forms of authoritarianism and for its commitment to decentralized forms of organization. However, this strategy does not challenge fundamental structures of power directly, because it does not suggest a way to bring these multiple TAZs and struggles together in a democratic way to collectively craft a vision of a free society. Nor does it offer a plan to defeat the massive resources of the powers that presently be.

The ineffectiveness of these two strategies requires a different response. This third response, revolutionary pluralism, is the position Love and Rage has finally arrived at after six years of debate and struggle. It is based on our perception of what a 21st century mass movement against oppression will look like. While movements aimed at organizing workers in factories and in socialist political parties may have been appropriate in the late 19th and early 20th centuries, the ever-changing landscape of capital and imperialism has grown much more diverse and complex today. The mass movements against them will inevitably reflect this diversity and complexity. The proletariat is no longer the sole agent of revolutionary potential. The struggles of women, people of color, and oppressed nationalities throughout the world are no longer secondary concerns but constitute the potential, in their plurality, to be the foundations for a new mass movement. What will bring this diverse, plural movement of movements and peoples together? Only a deliberate struggle to unite them into a democratic and plural movement can successfully challenge the existing power structure while maintaining the autonomy and integrity of these various movements.

If the mass movements of the 21st century are going to be plural, diverse, and from a variety of different sources, what is the role of a revolutionary organization in such a movement? Clearly such an organization cannot and should not attempt to make itself the "vanguard" of such a movement and try to force the entire movement to conform to its own ideology and become subordinate to its own organs of power. However, because the role of a vanguard organization has been thoroughly discredited, this does not mean that there is no role at all for revolutionary organization, as advocates of organic strategies argue. The role of a revolutionary anti-authoritarian organization (like Love and Rage) in a mass movement, is not to lead the movement but to participate in it as equals with other organizations and peoples. When participating in political movements, as individuals and as Love and Rage members, we argue for two things: 1) the most democratic mass movement possible, one that gives every person the ability to participate in it equally; and 2) our anti-authoritarian politics within this plural movement to influence it to struggling against all forms of oppression.

Of course, a plural and diverse mass movement does not exist in North America today. At present, groups like Love and Rage are organizations without a movement. We do not pretend to be able to be this movement nor to be able to create it ourselves. That is the work of millions of the downtrodden and oppressed. However, we can and do participate in small movements right now, with the eye toward not only winning these smaller struggles but also bringing them together into a larger, plural movement. We do this by actively participating in them and arguing for our positions in a free and open manner. Toward this end, Love and Rage sees three current struggles that are not yet mass movements but that hold great potential for inspiring mass political struggle in the near future. The struggle against white supremacy—not only against the far-right but also against the principal institutions of this society (cops, courts, capital)—will be key to any revolutionary movement. Secondly, the Zapatista uprising indicates that Mexico will be a central point for resistance to the global capitalist order in the upcoming century, and so we work to support our comrades in Mexico and to open up a "Northern Front" in the US and Canada. And finally, the criminalization of drugs, poverty, and welfare recipients means that we must focus attention on prisons and the criminal justice system, not only to support our revolutionary comrades held in prisons, but also to reveal prisons as the lynchpin of social control and as a key weapon of Black genocide under capitalism. Society will not be free until it is free of prisons. Revolutionary pluralism offers a guide to building this new world within the complex and confusing shell of the terrible world we live in now.

3

The Role of Structure and Organization in a Revolutionary Movement
By Matt Black
Love and Rage Editorial, May/June 1995

THE QUESTION, "WHAT IS THE ROLE OF structure and organization in a revolutionary movement?" has two aspects: "What is the role of structure?" and "What is the correct/appropriate structure?" I think that these two questions are really two sides of a more central question: "What are we trying to accomplish in the long run, and how is that affected by our structure?" On the most basic level, we are trying to change the world by building up a new society within the old, hoping that the new society will destroy the old one in the process. The editorial in the last issue of *Love and Rage* discussed why we need a structure/organization to do this. Here, I will try to sketch how we will do this.

ORGANIZATION IN GENERAL

In general, I think there are three main functions of organization. Organization is needed, first, to unify with people who are oppressed by, and in opposition to, this society; second, to connect with other people who are already insurgent against this society. Finally, organization can attempt to prefigure the new society by building new social and personal relations that embody, as much as possible, our vision of the new society. To me, the last is the most important function.

The purpose of unifying with people already in opposition is to show the connections among the various structures that oppress us and to see our opposition as part of a broader struggle. The purpose of connecting with people who are actively insurgent is to build coalitions and to become parts of those struggles. In both areas, we should be seeking to argue for our politics—both our analysis and our commitment to democracy, pluralism, and anti-authoritarianism. We should also seek to participate in movements that help us to see ourselves as interested in and capable of taking action to change our lives, so that we move from anger and resentment into opposition and revolt.

But the real core of our politics, I think, and what distinguishes us from other political forces, is in our commitment to building the new society now. This is central for two reasons. It (hopefully) allows us to see our work as part of the revolution instead of being prior to it; at the same time, the process of trying to build something new is what will really be the undoing of the old.

This is the major lesson that I have drawn from the EZLN. They went to Chiapas wanting two things: to make a revolution and to see their political ideas come true. As they struggled along with the people of Chiapas, who were already insurgent against the larger society, the Zapatistas discovered that their two goals were in conflict: the people in Chiapas wanted revolution, but not on the EZLN's terms. Then something mind-blowing happened: the EZLN effectively decided that it wanted revolution more than it wanted to be right. They began with the idea of descending on Chiapas and transforming it; instead, they were transformed along with it. At some point, the EZLN had to choose between the people and their abstract idea of revolution. They chose the people, only to discover (happily) that the people were the revolution.

Will we be as smart and courageous? I think we will in part, through the process of building revolutionary structures, including the Love and Rage Federation. But this will happen only if we develop a clear understanding of just what it is we are trying to do.

Our political perspective is anti-authoritarian for two reasons: first, we think that authority tends to create and perpetuate rigidly hierarchical social structures. Just as important, we think that authority serves to destroy the very quality that is necessary to make the new society: people's ability to act. Therefore, we try to structure our organizations to prefigure the new society. We don't do this because we are hopeless utopian romantics. Rather, as we fight to transform ourselves into people capable of acting, we truly begin to oppose this society and struggle for the new one.

Ultimately, I believe the insurgent social movements will be able to transform society. But this will happen only insofar as the members of those movements have created intentionally prefigurative structures and organizations, through which they themselves have been transformed.

4

Demise of the Beehive Collective: Infoshops Ain't the Revolution

BY BRAD SIGAL
LOVE AND RAGE, AUGUST/SEPTEMBER 1995

IN APRIL 1995, THE BEEHIVE COMMUNITY SPACE & INFOSHOP in Washington DC shut its doors. The Beehive Autonomous Collective started meeting in July 1993, and opened the infoshop in October 1993. This article will analyze some of what happened at Beehive and attempt to draw some lessons that might be useful for the infoshop movement and the anarchist movement in general. I was involved with Beehive for the entire lifespan of the group. In this article, I am only speaking for myself as one member of the project.

WHAT IS AN INFOSHOP?

An infoshop is a space where people involved with radical movements and counter-cultures can trade information, meet and network with other people and groups, and hold meetings and/or events. They often house "free schools" and educational work-shops. Infoshops have existed in Europe for decades. The Spanish revolutionary infoshops of the 1930s and the current European infoshops provided some of the inspiration for the newer North American infoshops.

THE NORTH AMERICAN INFOSHOP MOVEMENT

While a few bookstores/infoshops existed in the 1980s, the current wave of infoshops basically started in the aftermath of the Gulf War in 1991. Their growth was a direct response to frustrations some anarchists felt trying to organize a movement against the Gulf War without any institutions to draw upon or sustain day-to-day activism in our communities. The Long Haul infoshop in the Bay Area and the Emma Center in Minneapolis served as inspirations and models for some of the other infoshops. The more punk-music oriented spaces like Epicenter in San Francisco and Reconstruction Records in New York were also inspirations for some people.

ORIGINS OF BEEHIVE & DRAWING LESSONS

Like many of today's infoshops, Beehives' origins are in punk-rock counterculture. It developed out of the contradictions facing the DC punk community in 1993. Many people in the DC punk scene had been politically active since the mid-1980s and many of the more popular DC punk bands had political lyrics and played many ben-efit concerts during that time. While the benefit concerts have continued, by 1993 the tendency toward activism in the punk scene was fading. A few of us who had been involved in punk-oriented activist groups, such as Positive Force, Riot Grrrl and Food not Bombs, were feeling more isolated from the rest of the punk scene. We came together out of the experiences we had in these other groups, in a mostly unarticulat-ed attempt to move beyond the confines of the punk scene and to become more involved with and relevant to other DC communities. Others who hadn't been previously involved in DC punk/political groups also got involved—attracted to the concept of either a "free space," a record store, or a hangout space.

LITTLE PARTICIPATION FROM LOCAL COMMUNITY

One of the most noticeable things about Beehive's beginning was that almost all of the people who got involved were not from DC—even further, many people had just recently moved to DC. Only a few people who were ever involved with Beehive actually grew up in the DC area or had lived there more than a couple of years. This helped produce a larger problem—none of the people in the collective were from the particular neighborhood where we opened our infoshop, and we never succeeded in attracting neighborhood residents to the project.

When Beehive was starting out, the fact that so many people were from out of town was refreshing, as it strengthened the waning "political" tendency in the DC punk scene. But in retrospect, it was a weakness that caused a continual shortsightedness and contributed to the group's end.

This "transient" tendency isn't surprising considering the social base Beehive came out of. The punk scene is generally young, politically inexperienced, and has very high turnover. There is a strong commitment to individual and/or spontaneous acts of creativity (bands, fanzines, fashion, etc.) but a non-committal or skeptical attitude toward organized movements or organizations. To start a community-based organization such as an infoshop, however, requires long-term thinking and commitment. This basic tension—between the attention span and commitment level of our social base, and the commitment level necessary to do what we said we wanted to do—was a problem in Beehive from beginning to end.

DOMINANCE OF PUNK-ROCK CULTURE

The fact that Beehive came out of the punk-rock community isn't inherently bad by any means. But we need to recognize the limitations of the punk scene and how those limitations make a community organizing project very difficult, if not impossible.

At Beehive, we also experienced the strange tendency for punk to dominate all that it comes in contact with. While Beehive was started by punks, some non-punk anarchists and other activists were attracted to it at first. But none of the non-punk activists stayed involved, and it wasn't until that last few months of the group that a few non-punk anarchists got involved. While the non-punks who left had their individual reasons for leaving the group, I think, in most cases, it was partly related to the dominance of punk in the group.

Since the visible activities happening at Beehive were punk-related, more middle class punks continued to be attracted to the project, mostly from outside of DC. So we were continually treading water, always saying we wanted to "get beyond" the punk community and interact with and involve people from the neighborhood around us, but continually attracting more and more punks (with varying degrees of commitment to community organizing). This further strengthened the association of Beehive with the punk scene and made it increasingly more difficult to attract other communities to the project.

The answer to this question is not easy, as punk has probably done more than anything else in the last twenty years to popularize anarchism and to articulate the anti-authoritarianism of alienated white youth. Punk culture should exist and thrive in radical spaces, but it shouldn't dominate.

There is an underlying strain of arrogance and elitism to much of punk culture—a belief that "the masses are asses" or that everyone else is just stupid and conforms to society's expectations. Also, the fact that punks tend to come from white, middle-class backgrounds means that many punks have more resources and money at their disposal to develop their projects than people from more working-class counter-cultures. This factor makes it easy for punk to unintentionally dominate a space. Many punks receive "hidden" support from parents and middle-class jobs which allow more punk bands to buy nicer equipment, put out their own records, tour more easily, etc.

GENTRIFICATION

When we started looking for a building to move our community space into, we were immediately confronted with the high cost of rent in DC. The cheapest rent we were able to find somewhat near a subway station and somewhat near where most of us lived was in a neighborhood that is in the process of gentrification.

Gentrification is the process by which a working-class or poor-urban neighborhood starts to become desirable to middle-class or yuppie people ("gentry") from outside of that neighborhood. One of the main desirable factors is the cheap rent. Once middle-class people move in, they start to make "improvements," demand more police presence to protect their property, and businesses start to appear to cater to their middle-class and yuppie tastes. As the neighborhood becomes more "desirable" for people with money, property values start to rise, and the original poor or working-class residents of the neighborhood can't keep up with the rising costs and have to move out. It is a process of colonization on a smaller level.

Some of us repeatedly raised the issue of gentrification in the group while we were deciding where to locate our infoshop. We were conscious of our role as outsiders to the U Street neighborhood we were considering, and we were wary of the "revitalization" going on a few blocks down the street. The U Street & 14th Street corridors were burned out in April 1968 in the urban uprisings after Dr. Martin Luther King was assassinated. Until the early '90s, the commercial corridors remained partly vacant while surrounding neighborhoods suffered from the violence and decay that has wreaked havoc on inner cities over the past thirty years.

Around when we were looking at the neighborhood, a group of new "hip" businesses had joined together to market the concept of "The New U," which was used in ads in citywide papers to try to attract outsiders to come shop the new U Street businesses. The "New U" businesses down the street hit a nerve with us because many of them were started by people from our community—punks and alternative types. Since they were from our community, we wanted to differentiate from them, but in reality we didn't really know how.

We didn't want to contribute to the gentrification process, although none of us had a clear idea of how to oppose it. We agreed that we would try to be different than the stores of "The New U" down the street. We would be different because we would try to serve needs of people who lived in the neighborhood (through free clothing, free food, and free daycare programs, for example) rather than trying to bring in yuppies from outside with money. We knew we would make mistakes, but we didn't see ourselves contributing to gentrification as long as we were actively struggling against it politically. Gentrification turned out to be one of the two major divisive issues in Beehive, and it seems to be that way at most infoshops around the US.

INTERNAL GROUP DYNAMICS: RACE, CLASS & GENDER

Other than gentrification, it was internal group dynamics centering on race, class, and gender that were the most pressing and most divisive issues that Beehive faced. This also seems to mirror the experience of other infoshops around the US. We had a series of internal conflicts which escalated in intensity, until May, 1994, when two members and two non-members of the group confronted the rest of the group in a very abrasive way for what they saw as sexism, classism, and racism in the way the group operated. Those of us involved in Beehive learned a lot from these internal struggles. It forced us to confront many of our personal motivations and approaches, to try to figure out which of our actions came out of our genuinely progressive aspirations, and which came from our culturally brainwashed upbringing in a white-supremacist, patriarchal, and capitalist society.

Unfortunately, some who supported Beehive but weren't directly involved seemed turned-off or intimidated by the perceived hostile infighting. This further isolated us from the community that we originally emerged from. More importantly, I think these internal struggles happened in a way that was disconnected from any practice of trying to change oppressive institutions in society and without seeing that our mistakes were not just due to individual shortcomings but were being replicated by many other groups at the same time. Although it wasn't easy to see at the time, the struggles over internal dynamics in the group escalated precisely when it became clear that Beehive wasn't accomplishing the political goals that we claimed to aspire to. The free daycare never happened. A proposal for a community-organizing project was passed but then never acted on. Anti-gentrification discussion and efforts were pushed into the background. Other activist groups weren't using Beehive as a meeting space or resource center. The lending library was falling apart.

This wasn't because we didn't care about these things anymore. We just hadn't realized how much work it would take just to maintain and staff the infoshop, let alone actually using it as a base from which to launch activist projects. Once we had rented a building and moved in, it took all our energy (and then some!) just to staff and open the infoshop three days a week (we would have liked to have been open every day). Repairs to the building were never made. Bureaucratic paperwork with the government to make our infoshop "legal" was never filled out—partly because we decided not to, but even if we had wanted to, we just weren't organized enough to handle it.

Among the people who were consistently involved with the group, many of us traveled for weeks or months at a time and our involvement varied accordingly. Core people moved away from DC at a few key moments in the group's history. There was never a clear sense that people would be around very long. This "come and go" situation among core members and the high turnover among others made it impossible to progress on internal group dynamics. For example, at a meeting one week, a woman would confront the group about sexism, and we would agree to spend the next meeting discussing the situation in depth. Then at the next meeting, there would only be a few people there who were at the previous meeting. Everyone else there missed "the incident" and had no idea what was happening or why it was suddenly so urgent to spend the whole meeting talking about our sexism. The discussions on internal dynamics would mostly consist of uncomfortable silence. The people who brought the issue up in the first place would say what they thought, and there would be some hesitant discussion, but real group dialogue on these issues almost never happened. We just weren't able to handle it as a group.

Transience makes it impossible to deal with internal dynamics. To get anywhere on such issues, I think a group needs to have a somewhat stable membership who can work out interpersonal dynamics over time, and the group also needs to be actively struggling to bring about change outside of itself. Otherwise, dealing with internal dynamics becomes all-consuming and becomes more like group therapy than struggling to change the society we live in.

Some people attracted to counter-institutions act in oppressive ways (intentionally or unintentionally) and take up more than their share of the group's time in dealing with their personal problems or idiosyncrasies. I don't think we should be afraid of criticizing or "alienating" people who detract from the focus of the group or make others feel uncomfortable. I think we need to commit ourselves to finding ways to deal seriously with oppressive aspects of our group dynamics in a way that encourages people to speak, grow, and learn to become better activists through experience and comradely criticism.

NO UNIFYING VISION, NO CLEAR GOALS, NO STRATEGY

The other missing link in dealing with internal dynamics is a clear sense of vision in the group. If everyone involved is clear about the purpose of the group (i.e. if the purpose and goals are worked out at the beginning and clarified into a written statement), then the group can always refer back to that to see if its outward activities and internal dynamics are actually helping to fulfill those goals or not. But with Beehive, and I think many other infoshops too, we never truly had political agreement on what our goals and purpose were.

We did have a statement of purpose, but it was crafted in a carefully vague way to allow for anything and avoid making choices about a specific course of action. We defined Beehive as "an all-volunteer collective promoting communication through books, records, 'zines, performance meetings, and social/political networking. In our attempt to break the cycle of an historically classist, sexist, racist, heterosexist and authoritarian social system, we feel it is imperative to oppose capitalist oppression. It has denied us self-realization and free association. Beehive intends to bridge the ever increasing gap between privilege and underdevelopment by providing access to space and information at low cost or free. We will: be organic, radical, wild, and revolutionary; creative and critical, locally and internationally."

When you take away what we are abstractly for and against, that leaves only promoting communication and providing a space for other people to "do their own thing." While these are good things to do, they do not differ fundamentally from what the public library does, for example. And I would argue in the current context, at least in DC, they are not the most valuable use of our energies in building a revolutionary anti-authoritarian movement.

While our statement took some political stands (against capitalism, racism, sexism, and heterosexism), we did not have a political focus of our own to fight against those things. By coming out against those things politically, while having no program to work against them, we were setting ourselves up to be torn apart by struggles over those oppressions in the internal dynamics of the group—and that's exactly what happened. This shows why it is important to have an agreed upon purpose for the group, as well as an attempt to create a strategy to realize those goals.

Having no agreed upon purpose creates one set of problems that will probably lead to misunderstandings and frustration, factionalism, and people leaving the group confused and frustrated about what the group is supposed to be doing. Having a unified purpose but no strategy creates another similar set of problems, which will often cause people to become frustrated and look to each others' individual shortcomings for the source of the problem, rather than trying to create a strategy to have an effect on the world around us. Most infoshops seem to be stuck in one or the other of these problems; Beehive was usually somewhere in between.

THE UNSTATED (DIS)IDEOLOGY OF INFOSHOPS

While Beehive's political statement avoided articulating a specific strategy or focus, we were still following an unspoken strategy. The failure to articulate a strategy doesn't mean that you don't have one, it just means that you haven't consciously worked through it as a group. I think most infoshops try to take the easy way out of developing and implementing a strategy to reach our stated ideals, by stating our purpose simply as sharing information and providing a space for people to use. This creates a big gap between our stated goals (against capitalism, racism sexism, heterosexism) and our actual activities (educational and logistical support work). We had revolutionary ideas but little strategy to work toward realizing them.

COUNTER-INSTITUTIONS AS "THE REVOLUTION"

As you can probably tell by now, I don't see infoshops or counter-institutions as "the answer" or "the strategy" for building a revolutionary anarchist movement. I do, however, think that they can be an important part of a strategy if there is a mass movement to support and sustain them. Some people (though probably not many in the anarchist-infoshop movement) do see counter-institutions as "the revolution." Their strategy basically says that through creating non-profit cooperatives (food co-ops, free medical clinics, housing co-ops, etc.) we will set examples of a different type of society and serve the needs of our communities, which others will then copy. The counter-institutions will continue to gain power and will be able to serve the needs of the people, making the current power structures irrelevant without having to struggle directly against them.

What this strategy leaves out is that the institutions in power have an interest in staying in power and will fight to preserve and expand their power. They will struggle directly against our counter-institutions whether we fight them or not. So without a means to directly confront them, our counter-institutions will be crushed when they are perceived as enough of a threat to the status quo.

However, in the current political context (without strong mass movements), the greater danger to counter-institutions is of being co-opted into a harmless "alternative," without revolutionary context. We can see this in many food co-ops that started in the co-op surge of the early 1970s and which are now catering increasingly to a yuppie clientele and adopting more of a capitalist approach. I think this shows that counter-institutions are not inherently revolutionary. They can go in many directions.

COUNTER-INSTITUTIONS AS A FOUNDATION FOR REVOLUTIONARY GROWTH?

A more developed analysis sees infoshops not as inherently revolutionary, but as one part of a revolutionary strategy. As Jacinto from Chicago's Autonomous Zone infoshop wrote in the first issue of *(dis)connection*, "the revolution is not in the formation of these counter-institutions but in the revolutionary potential of the collectives which can use the resources provided by liberated spaces." Jacinto argues that building sustainable radical counter-institutions now will provide a launching pad for all sorts of radical projects and collectives. This strategy makes sense. It sees the need for building ongoing institutions to sustain radical activism, and it also sees the limitations of those counter-institutions by themselves. This strategy says that the missing ingredient—the reason there are not more radical projects and collectives—is that there is not a base of support, information, and resources for such projects to develop. According to this strategy, if we build infoshops as that base, then the amount of activist projects in our community should grow.

This was the unstated strategy that I was pursuing through Beehive, and I think it's the unstated strategy of a lot of people who are involved in infoshops. While this strategy sounds good, it did not work in practice for us, and I don't see much evidence of it working elsewhere. One possibility is that Beehive did not survive long enough to "bear fruit" in the form of new projects and collectives. But as it was, our whole group was drained just keeping the Beehive infoshop afloat and staffed from week to week. The anarchist and radical communities are just too small in DC to sustain an anarchist infoshop and to also develop other projects. Rather than building the basis for further growth of radical projects, my experience is that infoshops will burn out the core group of activists and thus prevent them from developing or contributing to new projects.

WHERE TO GO FROM HERE: REVOLUTIONARY PLURALISM & INFOSHOPS AS A PART OF A REVOLUTIONARY STRATEGY

This is the situation we find ourselves in—in North America in 1995, we are trying to build a revolutionary anti-authoritarian movement on almost no solid foundation. Many young anarchists realize that we need ongoing institutions to sustain our work during the high points and low points of mass movements. Over the past few years, many of us have tried to build local infoshops and community centers to fulfill that function.

At best, the results have been mixed. Most of the infoshop collectives have attracted new people to anarchist politics and have given anarchists an ongoing project that has the potential to deal with daily issues faced by oppressed and alienated people. Some of the infoshops have improved the reputation of anarchists in their cities by being a visible example of their politics, while a couple have also taken militant direct action on neighborhood issues such as gentrification.

At the same time, every infoshop I know has experienced severe internal problems, with serious factional fights and with many people leaving infoshops frustrated, angry, or burnt out. The factional fights and splits have escalated to vandalism or threats of violence at places like Emma Center in Minneapolis, Beehive in DC, and Epicenter in San Francisco.

While much of the initial point of starting infoshops was to create a stable, ongoing presence in a particular city or community, some infoshops which opened with lofty expectations are already closed, such as Croatan in Baltimore and Beehive in DC. Other infoshops that are still open have already had to move once or twice like Chicago's A-Zone. And of all the infoshops I'm familiar with, I can't think of any that have helped facilitate the starting of new projects or collectives except as hostile splits from the infoshop collective! Other projects that have developed probably would have formed anyway without the existence of the infoshops.

In cities where active anarchist projects and collectives already exist, it might make sense to set up an infoshop. But generally, infoshops haven't been very successful at supporting and helping develop new projects. I think this is because of a lack of open discussion about our politics, vision, and strategy. While skills-sharing is crucial to helping disempowered and alienated people take control over their lives, I think the "missing ingredient" in the lack of new anarchist projects is our lack of political vision for the future and our lack of developing realistic strategies to move toward that vision. Can we really consider infoshops a cornerstone of a revolutionary movement if we can't have a discussion about anything deeper than what color to paint the room without causing a major split in the collective?

To deal with these questions, I think we need to take a step back from the specific political projects (such as infoshops) that we've chosen to work on. I don't mean to say that we should abandon such projects, but that they are bound to fail unless we simultaneously take a step back and build stable, ongoing political collectives, organizations, or other forums, as a political infrastructure for our movement. The focus of such organization should be specifically to develop political vision and strategy, and hence work to implement that strategy. These can be local, regional, national, or international groupings. Love and Rage is one example of such a group, but there are many such organizations with varying visions and strategies that will be part of any revolutionary movement. This is what I think of when I think of "revolutionary pluralism."

Infoshops may be one aspect of a political strategy that such political groupings could develop. But infoshops aren't a strategy in themselves and are failing as a shortcut for working through our political differences and coming up with coherent visions and strategies to realize an anarchist future. I don't think that it's a mistake to work on infoshops and I wouldn't say that the two years working on Beehive were a waste of time (to the extent that we are willing to admit our shortcomings, honestly sum up that experience to learn from it, and move forward). This article is my attempt to do that and my view is that it's time to work on other projects instead of starting another infoshop.

RACE

1

To Advance the Class Struggle, Abolish the White Race

By Noel Ignatiev

Love and Rage, November/December 1994

Race is a biological fiction, but it is a social fact. The white race consists of those who enjoy the privileges of white skin—freedom from unreasonable searches and seizures, the inside track for jobs and careers, not having to fear for their lives every time they leave the home, expecting, if they are female, that the state will protect them from strangers. Its most downtrodden members enjoy a social status above any person defined as "non-white."

From the standpoint of the working class, the white race is an attempt by some workers to cut a separate deal with capital, at the expense of the class of which they are a part. From the standpoint of capital, it is a cheap way of buying some loyalty to a social system that exploits them.

The cops provide an example of how the white race is held together: the natural attitude of the police toward the exploited is hostility. All over the world, cops beat up poor people, and it has nothing to do with color. What is unusual and has to be accounted for, is not why they beat up Black people, but why they don't normally beat up propertyless whites. The cops look at a person and decide on the basis of color whether that person is loyal to, or an enemy of, the system they are sworn to serve and protect. They don't stop to think if the Black person whose head they are whipping is an enemy; they just assume it. It does not matter if the victim goes to work every day, pays taxes, and crosses only on green.

On the other hand, the cops don't know for sure if the white person to whom they give a break is loyal to them. They assume it. The non-beating for whites is time for good behavior and assurances of future cooperation. White workers' color exempts them to some degree from the criminal class—which is how the entire working class was defined before the invention of race, and is still treated in those parts of the world where race does not exist as a social category.

How to Abolish the White Race

But what if the police couldn't tell a loyal person just by color? What if there were enough people around who looked white but were real enemies of the state so that the cops couldn't tell whom to beat and whom to let off? What would they do then? They would begin to "enforce the law impartially" as the liberals say. But, as Anatole France noted, "The law, in its majestic equality, forbids both rich and poor to sleep under bridges, to beg in the streets, to steal bread." The standard that governs police behavior all over the world (except where race exists) is wealth and its external manifestations: dress, speech, etc. At the present time, the class bias of the law is partially repressed by racial considerations; the removal of those considerations would give it free rein. White poor would find themselves on the receiving end of police justice as Black people do now. The effect on their consciousness and behavior is predictable.

The abolitionists consider it a useless project to try to win the majority of whites, or even the majority of working-class whites to "anti-racism." They seek instead to compel capital to turn millions of "whites" against it, by rendering white skin useless as a predictor of attitudes. How many would it take to rob the white skin of its predictive value? No one can say. How much counterfeit money has to circulate in order to destroy the value of the official stuff? The answer is nowhere near a majority: in the past, five to ten percent fake has proven enough to undermine public faith in the other. Whiteness is the currency of this society; to destroy it would take only enough counterfeit whites (race traitors) to undermine the confidence of the police, etc. in their ability to differentiate between friends and enemies by color.

The abolitionist strategy depends on the coming together of a minority determined to break up the white race. What would the determined minority have to do to plant doubt about the reliability of white skin? They would have to break the laws of whiteness so flagrantly as to make it impossible to maintain the myth of white unanimity. Such actions would jeopardize their own ability to draw upon the privileges of whiteness. That is what would define them as race traitors.

Just as the capitalist system is not a capitalist plot, race is not the work of racists. On the contrary, it is reproduced by the principal institutions of society. Therefore, the main target of those who seek to eradicate it should be the institutions and behaviors that maintain it: the schools (which define 'excellence'), the unions and employers (which define 'employment'), the justice system (which defines 'crime'), the welfare system (which defines 'poverty'), and the family (which defines 'kinship').

AGAINST FASCISM, AGAINST CAPITAL, AGAINST THE STATE

The collapse of the white race does not mean that all people now classified as white would suddenly become revolutionary. Some, whose class interests rest on exploitation, would remain faithful to the capitalist system. However, once color ceased to serve as a handy guide for deciding who gets a beating and who gets off, many victims would join with the rest of the working class in waging a struggle against capital.

Others would take a different path, seeking to restore the privileges of the white race. Alongside the class struggle, it is to be expected that militant white-supremacist movements with anti-capitalist slogans would grow among the poorest and most alienated sectors of white society.

The fascists are the vanguard of the white race; however, the big problem right now is not the white vanguard but the white mainstream. Any anti-fascist struggle that does not confront the state reinforces the institutions that provide the seedbed for fascism. Moreover, every time the fascists are able to depict their opponents as defenders of the existing system, or mere reformers, they gain support among those whites who believe that nothing less than a total change is worth fighting for. An anti-fascist counter-rally where people gather to hear speeches, chant slogans, and shake their fists in rage, is a display of impotence, and the more people who attend, the more they reveal their futility.

Fascism and white supremacy will only be defeated by a movement aimed at building a new world. It is not enough to declare this commitment abstractly, by waving the red or black flag; it must be expressed in the content and forms of the struggle itself. How to do that is no easy question. But it is the question of the hour.

Noel Ignatiev is one of the editors of Race Traitor: A Journal of the New Abolitionism. *Subscription information can be obtained by writing PO Box 603, Cambridge, MA 02140-0005.*

[Note from the Production Group: The women of the PG strongly disagree with Noel's statement at the outset of this article "not having to fear for their lives every time they leave the home, expecting that…the state will protect them from strangers" is a "social fact" for white women. As white women, we have all been harassed by the police and fear that we will fall victim to the common practice of police rape and a legal system that makes it nearly impossible for a woman to 'prove' she has been raped. Some of us have been physically abused in the presence of police that have turned the other way.

Given that this is the only reference Noel makes to women in his article, on class struggle and white privilege, we gave him the opportunity to delete the sentence. He refused, arguing that it is his viewpoint and that it should be left in to "provoke debate." We find the claim offensive, and we want to point out that we believe it runs contrary to the newspaper's commitment to recognizing the way in which state power is used to uphold patriarchy.]

2

Building a Multi-Racial/Mulit-National Revolutionary Anarchist Organization

Love and Rage Editorial, June/July 1997

WE CANNOT IMAGINE AN ANARCHIST REVOLUTION in the United States that is not multi-racial and multi-national. White supremacy is so central to the workings of US society that a movement that does not involve the full participation of the masses of Black, Latino, Asian, and Native peoples cannot realize our vision of a free society. Accordingly, if Love and Rage is to carry out the tasks that we believe are required of a revolutionary anarchist organization, we must become a multi-racial/multi-national organization.

An organization that does not have deep roots in the communities of all oppressed peoples cannot hope to develop a revolutionary theory and practice that can win real freedom for all people. Only a multi-racial/multi-national organization can hope to develop the collective political perspective necessary to take on the system we are up against. We do not want to be a multi-racial/multi-national organization just to make ourselves feel good, but rather because we believe this is a prerequisite for making revolution in this country. Building such an organization is profoundly different and more difficult than just participating in or building multi-racial or multi-national mass movements. To do so we must confront a number of difficult issues.

With a few exceptions, the experiences of predominantly white organizations seeking to transform themselves into multi-racial and multi-national organizations has not been a good one. The recurrent spectacle of self-appointed white vanguards bringing the "correct line" to people of color has given rise to a legitimate skepticism on the part of many activists of color about the project of building multi-racial/multi-national formations. If our efforts are to succeed, we must be willing to learn as well as teach.

An alternative to building multi-racial/multi-national organizations is the idea of an alliance of organizations, each based among different racial or national groups. While we uphold the right and necessity of oppressed peoples to form their own organizations, we do not think these should be the only type of organizations that should be built. We believe that large numbers of white people will need to participate in any successful social revolution in this country. This can only happen if the deeply-held loyalties to white power and privilege are broken. As history has taught us, it's been the struggles of people of color that have fractured the allegiances of whites to the system of white supremacy. It has been in multi-racial/multi-national organizations that the best fighters against white supremacy among white people have been schooled.

While we recognize the deep roots white supremacy has in the consciousness of most white people, we do not believe that only a handful of exemplary white people can be won to fighting white supremacy. We believe an end to this whole rotten system is in the ultimate interests of the vast majority of humanity, including the majority of white people. Accordingly, we reject the notion of the "white solidarity organization" that acts under the leadership of this or that people of color organization. The abdication of white people of the responsibility of thinking for themselves does not magically erase the colonial dynamic that exists between white people and people of color. The evasion of struggle over questions of principle for fear of being unpopular or criticized by people of color can only be called the politics of guilt. Moreover, the decision to take leadership from a particular organization is itself an intervention in the internal affairs of the community in which the organization is based. There is no escape from the logic of this society other than a revolutionary commitment to change it.

Since its founding, Love and Rage has had a number of experiences that have taught us valuable lessons about what it means to try to become a truly multi-national organization. We have committed both of the kinds of mistakes discussed above, and we are still not the kind of organization we want to be. With the notable exception of our Mexican section, we remain a mostly white and middle-class organization.

While we recognize that we still have much to learn from many different struggles, we do not think the main obstacle to winning people of color to Love and Rage is our internationalism, our anarchism, or our criticisms of any kind of nationalism. Our biggest obstacle is that Love and Rage is still culturally very white and therefore not the most immediately inviting place for people of color. Many Love and Rage members came to revolutionary anarchist politics through the punk and alternative music scenes, which, in the United States at least, are overwhelmingly white. People of color who join Love and Rage today will do so because of our politics and despite our perceived whiteness. Smashing this culture of whiteness is a major task in becoming the kind of truly inclusive organization we are committed to building.

We have been deeply influenced by many national liberation struggles in the Third World and the revolutionary nationalism of people of color organizations in North America. But we are not nationalists, and we have criticisms of many people we respect and admire in struggle. To us the historical record is clear: nationalism does not offer an adequate program for human liberation and in too many instances, so-called revolutionary nationalism has provided justification for the maintenance of systems of oppression. And in an increasingly globalized culture and economy we question whether national liberation struggles will occupy the central place in the world-wide struggle for freedom that they have for the past century.

We support the right of all oppressed peoples to self-determination. This means the right to choose between full political separation or simply autonomous cultural and community organizations. We do not believe that building a multi-racial/multi-national organization is in contradiction with this principle. In practice, the freedom to fully exercise this right of self-determination can only be won through a revolution involving people of every race and nationality.

The people of all colors who are most likely to be drawn to Love and Rage will be those who have been influenced to one degree or another by revolutionary nationalism but who reject that nation-state and who have embraced a broader politics that doesn't subordinate questions of gender, sexuality, or class to those of race and nation.

Smashing white supremacy and white privilege is a priority for Love and Rage. We see the project of building a multi-racial and multi-national revolutionary, anarchist organization as a necessary part of that fight. We understand that in order to become such an organization, we will have to go through some serious changes. We know these changes will not all be easy. We are fighting 500 years of racist history. We know that our responsibility is not merely to diversify our membership but to transform ourselves as individuals and as an organization. Because we are revolutionaries, we have faith that this can be done.

3

Response to Multi-Racial Organization Editorial

BY JOEL OLSON
LOVE AND RAGE, NOVEMBER/DECEMBER 1997

THE EDITORIAL "BUILDING A MULTI-RACIAL/MULTI-NATIONAL Revolutionary Anarchist Organization" in the June/July Love and Rage, and the defense of it in the August/September Love and Rage by eight New York Love and Rage members may give readers the impression that the Love and Rage Federation has a unified position on questions of race and activism and that the editorial accurately expresses that opinion. This is not the case. The editorial unfortunately presents only one perspective within the Federation, a perspective that I, as a long-time member of Love and Rage, believe is fundamentally wrong.

The editorial suffers from three crucial political errors. First, it has the relationship between fighting white supremacy and building a multi-racial organization backwards. Second, the publication of the editorial was undemocratic because it was published without significant debate by the membership. Finally, the politics expressed in the editorial lead us away from revolutionary action.

The editorial attempts to address several important questions that all revolutionaries must answer: how can we overcome the problem of a working class disastrously divided by the tragic history of white supremacy? What is the appropriate role of mostly-white revolutionary organizations in relating to communities and revolutionaries of color (who aren't already members of these organizations)? How should a mostly-white revolutionary organization proceed if it is to smash its whiteness and effectively tremble the pillars that prop up this evil system? Unfortunately, the solution the editorial provides for these questions—build a multi-racial organization—is a disastrous one. It is disastrous because, despite its good intentions, it objectively promotes a policy of white vanguardism. In making a call for people of color to join Love and Rage, the editorial essentially calls for a tiny, mostly-white organization to provide leadership for communities of color, particularly the Black community. This is vanguardism, which as anarchists we should absolutely avoid. We shouldn't be scrambling to put together a multi-racial organization to fight white supremacy but rather doing the reverse: struggling relentlessly and unceasingly against white skin privilege. Once we have proven ourselves as serious opponents of white privilege, we make it possible for Love and Rage to eventually become thoroughly multi-racial.

I also disagree that the reason Love and Rage is currently a mostly-white organization is because of "cultural reasons." Look at the rest of the American left: is it disproportionately white for "cultural reasons," too? Obviously not, but if other left groups have political problems that explain their general whiteness, how have we managed to avoid such errors while still remaining largely white? I agree that Love and Rage's political and social culture is not that comfortable for many people of color (nor for some of its present members!), but claiming that culture is the main obstacle preventing us from becoming multi-racial is a weak attempt to avoid the responsibility of examining the political principles that help keep us majority-white.

At this point in our history, it is not our job to meddle in the business of communities of color. Now, this could change. Love and Rage may grow to become a group with a significant Black, Latino, Asian, and/or Native-American membership. If this happens, then we can democratically decide, as a group, whether and when to begin taking positions on affairs concerning communities of color. But this is my second criticism of the editorial: if we're going to involve ourselves in issues that belong to communities of color (because we are or want to become a multi-racial group), we need to decide this democratically, after a full and free debate among all the membership. This has never happened yet. Thus, the position the "Building" editorial takes is undemocratic because it takes a position that the Love and Rage membership has not significantly debated nor voted on.

As a former member of Love and Rage's coordinating committee, I know how hard it is for a directly democratic organization to publish editorials. They have to reflect the politics of an organization whose principles and positions are still being developed and whose members are a pack of stubborn sonofaguns. I don't expect all members to proofread every editorial before it goes to print, but I do expect there to be prior federation-wide political discussion on issues before we put something in print, and that positions taken in editorials are unquestionably majority positions within the organization. I also expect our editorials to reflect our debates, including noting dissenting opinions when they exist.

Finally, I worry that the politics of the editorial, should they become the standard within Love and Rage, will lead us way from our commitment to revolution. As an organization of revolutionaries, the main point of our collective activism should be to develop and encourage campaigns and actions that work toward the building of a dual power. A dual power means that our strategies, tactics, and programs must directly challenge the existing institutions of power in this world and in some way prefigure the new society we want to build. I believe that any campaign or working group Love and Rage builds should be based on a dual power strategy, and that if a campaign or working group isn't, it should either be modified so that it is, or abandoned for another project. Strategies that are not based on dual power may achieve important social reforms, such as welfare reform, the establishment of civilian review boards for police, etc., but they don't threaten the system itself. As revolutionaries, we want to win reforms, of course, but not when they strengthen the hand of the state. We have to resist liberalism and the state at every moment and treat them as enemies just as much as the right.

I'm afraid that spending our time "building a multi-racial organization" rather than smashing the institutions that prop this evil system up—particularly the white race—will only continue our tendency to avoid the task of coming up with dual power strategies. In what ways do our three present working groups (anti-austerity, anti-fascist, anti-police) work to build a dual power? Do they work to abolish white skin privilege, or threaten the patriarchal family, or seek to disrupt other such institutions which are so crucial to the maintenance of this system? Or is their goal to make Love and Rage "multi-racial" through struggle and the winning of reforms?

I believe Love and Rage needs to reject the politics of the "Building" editorial and replace them with the following principles:

1) One of the key tasks of Love and Rage is to smash white power and white privilege wherever it appears, particularly in "normal" society .

2) A multiracial organization is a product of uncompromising struggle against white supremacy and white skin privilege—in society and within the organization—not the prerequisite of such struggle.

3) As an organization that is largely white and living in a white-supremacist socie-ty, we often unintentionally reproduce white power even as we fight against it. Therefore, Love and Rage must recognize that, at this time at least, our task is to abolish the white race and not to provide leadership for Black people or other communities of color.

The "Building" editorial, as far as I can tell, represents the politics of several comrades in Love and Rage. Probably others agree, but I have no way of knowing that. I hope and believe that many others disagree. I do know that the politics expressed in that editorial do not represent my views, and I urge the Federation, after a free and lively debate, to elect to print a retraction of "Building" in a future issue of the news-paper and to commit ourselves to grounding our activism in strategies of dual power.

In solidarity,
Joel Olson
Phoenix

4

Draft Resolution on White Supremacy

BY CHRIS (SAN CRISTOBAL), JESSICA (SAN CRISTOBAL), AND JOEL (PHOENIX)

LOVE AND RAGE CONFERENCE PAPER, 1997

THE PURPOSE OF THIS RESOLUTION is to clarify the position of Love and Rage on the white supremacist character of US society. It is to establish our position for the purposes of our mass work and to guide the Production Group in making editorial decisions regarding the political content of the newspaper.

1. The particular social structure of the United States is rooted in its history of conquest, colonization, genocide, and slavery and is distinguished by the system of white supremacy.

2. The foundation of the system of white supremacy is the system of white skin privilege, which grants significant material benefits to the white working class in exchange for its loyalty to the system as a whole. This system of white skin privileges has taken different forms over the course of US history but, it continues to function to this day.

3. These are not "petty" or "apparent" privileges, but rather significant concrete differences in the material conditions of life experienced by different sectors of a racially-divided working class. In many cases, these differences are matters of life and death, as is reflected in differences in infant mortality rates, life expectancy and causes of death between whites and people of color in general and Black people in particular.

4. Since the 1960s, a significant section of the Black community has been economically marginalized and excluded from the process of production. This section of the Black community is regarded by capital as intransigently rebellious and therefore disposable. The dramatic expansion of the prison system, the complete collapse of social services in urban centers, and policies that deliberately encourage the drug trade in the Black community constitute a pattern, that at the very least, has genocidal implications. The survival of the Black community in the US is threatened and must be defended.

5. The system of white skin privilege in the US is similar to the global inequalities that exist between the imperialist countries of Europe, North America, and Japan and the imperialized countries of Asia, Africa, and Latin America. These inequalities are reflected in a gulf between the standards of living of the workers of the imperialist countries and the workers and peasants of the imperialized countries.

6. Nevertheless, there are significant differences between the US racial system and global imperialism. Imperialism depends on colonial oppression, a system in which the ruling class of a colonized nation (a class which can be of any "race") rules for the benefit of the imperialist nation. On the other hand, white supremacy in the US depends on racial oppression, a system in which one section of the working class—whites—subordinates the rest of the working class for the benefit of capital and in exchange for material and psychological privileges. Thus, while a social hierarchy of the "white" race (however defined) over the "Black" or other "non-white"races (however defined) is a part of both colonial and racial forms of oppression; it operates differently in each form. The result is anti-colo-

nial national liberation struggle in imperialized countries and anti-racist struggle in the US.

7. The system of white skin privilege and the profound inequalities in the standards of living between the imperialist and imperialized countries constitutes the material foundation for the loyalty of white workers and workers in the imperialist countries to their respective ruling classes. This loyalty expresses itself as racism, imperialist patriotism, and as fascism under different circumstances.

8. Any revolutionary movement in the US must stand for the overthrow of the system of white skin privilege and the global system of imperialist privileges. This will mean a quantitative reduction in the standard of living for many workers in the imperialist countries in general and for white workers in the US in particular. Winning privileged workers to this necessity is a daunting but no less crucial aspect of revolutionary work in the US.

9. The white left in the US has historically ignored or denied the profound differences that exist between the material conditions facing white workers and Black workers. It has tended to fight for a program of "multi-cultural unity" or "Black and white unite and fight." The assumption of this program is that class unity and the improvement of the material conditions of people of color are best achieved by fighting for programs that raise up the conditions of "everyone" or "all workers" rather than strategies designed to specifically aid people of color, foster their self-determination, or abolish white privilege. This has been a tragic error of the American left. White privilege must be confronted directly, not subordinated to "more primary" matters of class. In the US at least, the struggle against white supremacy and for full Black social equality is not merely a prerequisite for working-class unity, in a certain sense it *is* the class struggle. When the walls of racial privilege tumble, the foundations of capital are threatened as well.

10. The struggle against white supremacy means supporting self-determination for Black people, Native peoples, Puerto Ricans, and Chicanos. This includes support for reparations. The principle of self-determination and the struggle for reparations by these and other oppressed communities must be respected by Love and Rage.

11. A still predominantly-white organization like Love and Rage must take this history of white leftists' chauvinism into account when it addresses questions of concern to the Black community and other communities of color. Love and Rage must scrupulously avoid the racist practice, followed by so many predominantly-white organizations, of attempting to provide leadership for Black and other liberation movements. The primary obstacle to multi-racial working class unity is white supremacy and not the narrow nationalist errors of this or that group based among racially or nationally oppressed peoples. Accordingly, our task now is to smash white supremacy, not criticize forces in racially oppressed communities. Therefore, public statements by Love and Rage members, particularly in the pages of our publications, should reflect the actual extent of our roots as an organization in those communities.

LOVE AND RAGE

1

Love and Rage Breaks Up

LOVE AND RAGE, FALL1998

AFTER MORE THAN EIGHT YEARS OF HARD WORK, the Love and Rage Revolutionary Anarchist Federation voted to dissolve itself during a brief conference at Hunter College in New York City on Saturday, May 23 1998. Some participants in the conference spent the rest of the weekend laying the foundation for a new provisional organization, the Fire By Night Organizing Committee. Members of another faction at the conference also announced their intention to launch a journal and a new organization. Neither of those projects has a name yet.

Love and Rage started out as a continental anarchist newspaper at a conference in Chicago back in 1989. The founding group included individuals and members of anarchist collectives from across the US and Canada, as well as an anarchist faction of the freshly-dissolved Trotskyist group, the Revolutionary Socialist League (RSL). Over the years, Love and Rage evolved from a loose network around the newspaper into a tighter organization. It became the Love and Rage Network in 1991 and the Love and Rage Revolutionary Anarchist Federation in 1993. This desire to build a serious and committed organization coupled with the involvement of the ex-RSL members made Love and Rage an object of continuous controversy within the anarchist scene. Despite these controversies, the reliable publication of the newspaper provided a valuable source of news and a forum for debate among anarchists and activists of many persuasions.

The break-up of Love and Rage was preceded by a two-year-long debate within the organization around a number of issues that proved irreconcilable. In the course of this debate, the ex-RSL members and a few others active in the Anti-Racist Action Network (ARA) signed onto a document titled What We Believe (WWB), which argued that all of the practical and theoretical problems that faced Love and Rage could be answered from "within anarchism." Other members raised provocative questions (How do you defend the ideals of a new society without replicating elements of a state? How does a revolutionary relate to her or his communities as an organizer?) and often found that anarchist history and thought didn t have satisfying answers. The WWB document and its backers offered vague and moralistic answers to such questions. Worse, WWB warned that this questioning was evidence of a covert plot to corrupt anarchism with Marxist thought.

A second major issue was the theory of white skin privilege, which holds that the material and psychological privileges granted to white people in the US, and not just racist ideology, is the primary obstacle to multi-racial unity among oppressed people in this country. WWB described the privileges granted to whites as "petty and apparent" and some members of the WWB faction attacked the theory of white skin privilege. In opposition to this position, others argued that opposition to the system of white skin privileges was central to their politics and part of what attracted them to Love and Rage in the first place.

A third major issue was practical work. Some of the WWB faction members had stopped doing any sort of mass organizing years ago. This was reflected in their politics. Some did political work locally, which often wasn't integrated into the Love and Rage Federation's strategic working groups. A couple were doing good work building ARA, but had failed to fulfill responsibilities to the organization which they had taken on when the Love and Rage Coordinating Committee (CC) was moved to their area. The CC was the body responsible for the day-to-day decision-making of Love and Rage, but this CC never met after it was elected at the 1997 Love and Rage Conference.

While this debate was taking place, two of the main Love and Rage locals broke down. The Minneapolis local became less and less active after several key members relocated to other cities and others came to see the organization as irrelevant to their work. The breakdown of the New York local came later and was more directly associated with the political divisions that finally split the organization.

Although many sought to keep the debate over these issues civil and focused on the underlying political questions, a number of documents sunk into personal attacks and distortions of people's actual political positions. It was in this context that many of the opponents of WWB decided that they could no longer remain in the same organization with the WWB faction. The degeneration of the debate combined with the organizational breakdown of the CC and several locals created a general demoralization that was followed by a rash of resignations from the organization, though these came primarily from members who had long been inactive.

It was clear that the organization had come to an impasse. Opponents of WWB realized that it was necessary to support a resolution to disband the organization, in order to clear the way for launching a new organization on a firmer foundation of political unity and commitment to actual participation in mass struggles.

This new organization took the name Fire By Night Organizing Committee from the Black spiritual *Go Down Moses* which refers to the use of "fire by night" to illuminate the route of the Underground Railway during slavery times. The name also reflects our desire to root our politics in the real traditions of struggle of the society we live in. In that spirit, we have decided to form a provisional committee that seeks to build an organization from the ground up with other groups and individuals we see as our political allies.

Several members of the new group still identify as anarchists, and the organization is committed to anti-authoritarian politics and an anti-statist revolutionary strategy. But we have deliberately chosen not to identify as an anarchist organization to make clear our anti-sectarianism, our openness to a range of political influences, and our determination to create a new revolutionary politics more in tune with the conditions of the 21st century. We look forward to continuing to work with all of our allies, both those who identify as anarchists and those who don't.

The Fire By Night Organizing Committee is currently composed of two local branches, one in New York City, and one in the San Francisco Bay Area. A number of other groups and individuals have already expressed interest in affiliating or working closely with the new organization. We will continue our participation in student and poor peoples' organizing efforts and we will carry out an intensive study and discussion process in order to clarify our basis for political unity. Fire By Night also plans to publish a critical evaluation of our experience in Love and Rage and a collection of documents from the debates that occurred over the past two years. There is a strong commitment on the part of its members that, in comparison to Love and Rage, the Fire By Night Organizing Committee will be more consistent in making sure that its members live up to expectations of membership that are appropriate to a serious revolutionary organization and that we will be more serious about the development of our politics through study, discussion and ongoing critical reflection on our experiences in mass organizing work.

The WWB faction has begun work on two projects. The first is a journal to be titled either *Liberty* or *Utopia* and to be produced by the ex-RSL members. The second is a call to form a Fresh Revolutionary Anarchist Group, "a federation of collectives united around firm anarchist/anti-authoritarian politics and outlook, oriented to the working classes and most oppressed and active in building Anti-Racist Action as an anti-authoritarian mass movement." Some members were unhappy with the lines along which the organization split and will not be part of any of the post-Love and Rage projects, nor will the small minority who actually did come to Marxist conclusions during the period of debate.

The final conference started civilly with reports on the work and future plans of the people in the room followed by a unanimous vote to disband Love and Rage. This tone was only broken when the question of dividing up the resources of the organization came up, and it became clear that the debts of the organization were greater than its assets. As it currently stands, the Fire By Night Organizing Committee has been shouldered with all of the debts incurred by Love and Rage. Negotiations are under way to see if the other projects will contribute anything to retiring Love and Rage's debts.

Members of Love and Rage expressed feelings ranging from deep sadness to profound relief at the disbanding of the organization. The burning question for members and non-members alike was what would happen to the newspaper, which was respected by many who never supported the organization that produced it. A final issue of the newspaper, which was almost ready to go to press at the time of the break-up conference, will be published. The Fire By Night Organizing Committee has decided not to publish a new publication for at least six months, to allow ourselves time to determine whether or not sufficient support exists for it and whether or not it is a politically appropriate use of our limited resources. We all appreciate the value of the newspaper, not just to ourselves but to the larger movement, and will be distressed if we end out choosing not to resume publication (under a new name of course).

2

What We Believe

LOVE AND RAGE *FEDERATION BULLETIN*, DECEMBER 1997

AS MEMBERS OF THE LOVE AND RAGE Revolutionary Anarchist Federation, we believe there is a need to restate some fundamental positions we hold in common. We have taken this step because some recent opinions stated within Love and Rage backtrack on some of these basic principles. We believe:

(1) Revolutionary anarchism is the program of a self-organized, cooperative, decentralized, and thoroughly democratic society. All social needs will be provided by a network of voluntary, self-managed associations. This means the overthrow of all forms of oppression, including, but not limited to, the domination of the working class, women, gays and lesbians, African Americans, Latinos, youth, neo-colonies, and nature. Self-organization of the people is both our vision of a new society and our program for reaching the new society.

(2) This makes anarchism central to our politics. There are historical failings of anarchism, but they can be dealt with from within anarchism. Anarchism's mistakes occur within a basically liberating vision. They include: (a) *ultimatism*, the idea that one can abstain from limited, reform struggles, (b) *anti-organizationalism*, opposition to organization, (c) *permeationism*, the idea that anarchist institutions can grow up within an authoritarian society and supplant it without a revolutionary struggle, and (d) *opportunism*, the idea (as in the Spanish revolution) that, under emergency conditions, one can join the state to defend it from anti-democratic enemies, instead of building an alternate to the state (such as federations of popular councils). The latter two, at least, show the attractiveness of authoritarianism, even to committed anarchists.

We must learn from other traditions of struggle, such as Black nationalism or feminism or ecology, but what we learn must be integrated into revolutionary anarchism. What matters is not anarchism as a label but anarchism as a vision and a program.

(3) Especially, Marxism should be seen as an opponent of anarchism. Whatever value its parts may have, Marxism was meant to be a total vision, a combination of economics, politics, historical analysis, and philosophy. This total vision is centralist and authoritarian to the core. Unlike the errors of anarchists, Marxism's "mistake," from our point of view, is basic to its real program, the creation of a new form of authoritarian state and society. It has produced pro-imperialist Social Democracy and the totalitarian state-capitalism of Stalinism. Ultimately, it can produce nothing else.

Despite historical defeats, Marxism remains a living danger. As radicalism increases, Marxism is likely to revive, due both to its strengths (its large body of theory and practice) and weakness (its authoritarianism, which many find attractive). Anarchists must work at analyzing, discussing, and refuting Marxism.

The impression that Marxism "works" because of China or Cuba or (retrospectively) Russia, and that anarchism does not "work" because it has never built a lasting free society, will be attractive to many. It is hard for people to believe in their own ability to create a new, just society, when states have been so successful in co-opting and crushing such efforts. Many find it easier to believe in authoritarianism because it seems to "work." Unfortunately, this lack of confidence may appear even among anarchists.

(4) The state should be replaced with a self-organized society—a federation of popular councils and committees and associations, such as have appeared in revolution after revolution. In place of the police and military would be the militia—the armed people. In the course of revolution and civil war, some repression and centralization may be temporarily necessary, but our principle is to limit it to the minimum which is absolutely necessary while encouraging as much freedom as is practically possible. There are some resemblances between a state and a self-organized people in a revolution, but they are not the same and must not become the same.

(5) Struggles for reforms should be supported whenever they mean real benefits, such as improving the popular standard of living, or expanding the area of freedom, or decreasing pollution. But these must be real benefits for the people, not just illusions. When we pose our reform demands, we do not worry about what the system can afford, but focus on what people need.

We will work with political groups with which we strongly disagree, for common reform goals. But we say that reforms are most likely won through the most militant mass actions, uniting as much of the oppressed as possible in independent opposition. We deny that improvements are won through elections, neither through the Democratic Party nor through a new progressive or labor party. We deny that liberation can be won by small bands of would-be heroes who take on the state, with guns and bombs by themselves, without the participation of the people.

Marxist-Leninists, nationalists, and others build organizations around the program of overthrowing the existing state and building new states. Regardless of personal motivation, such people are objectively working to create (and become) a new ruling class. We must struggle ideologically with them to break them from their ideas. We can and should bloc with revolutionary statists in common efforts, both for the immediate needs of the struggle and as a means to struggle against their ideas. We need to distinguish between hardened politicos who are not going to break with Marxism-Leninism for love or money and new or questioning people whom we can reach. Unfortunately, not everyone in Love and Rage seems to perceive the line of absolute difference in ultimate goals between us and many good activists who are objectively statist—or perceive the need to struggle against their statism.

Above all else, we tell people what we believe is the truth—about the limitations of reformist strategies and authoritarian leaders, and the need for a revolutionary anarchist strategy.

(6) The world is not divided into sectors, with anti-authoritarianism on the agenda in the advanced sectors but only nationalist capitalism on the agenda in the oppressed nations. We reject the political conclusions implied by this analysis, namely that one should work to establish progressive capitalist regimes in these less-favored sectors, and only fight to overthrow them later, if at all. Rather, we think:

a) Where nationalist or anti-imperialist revolts take place we should work for their victory while simultaneously trying to convince people to organize independently of the nationalists and to struggle to increase mass popular power before, during, and after these struggles. If it is not possible at a given point for popular organizations to realistically fight to replace the state, they should maximize their influence and prepare for the future. b) The idea of a distinct nationalist/anti-imperialist revolution has its own form in the advanced imperialist countries. Rather than separate stages of revolution, it implies separate struggles by different sectors such as African Americans and an alliance between anarchists and (whomever we think are) the leaders of these struggles. We believe in supporting just struggles, but criticizing authoritarian leaders. We organize people around libertarian and anarchist politics across color (and other) lines. c) Anarchism and not Marxism, has long been the best program for the liberation of humanity, in both the imperialist and the oppressed nations. We deny that supporting nationalist capitalists was correct in an earlier period but not today. This is a false distinction. The ultimate goal of an international non-state society seems just as far away today as fifty years ago in many countries, such as Palestine, South Africa, Congo, or Mexico. Consequently, the arguments for supporting nationalist capitalists are just as apparently persuasive, and just as dangerous to many people today.

(7) There is no one form of oppression (such as capitalism or racism) which underlies all others and is the most important. Nor are the separate oppressions just side-by-side. Rather, all forms of oppression are aspects of a single modern authoritarian system. For example, the struggle against capitalism is not just a matter for the working class as such, but is something in which women play a key role. The struggle against racism is not just a matter for African Americans, but requires the involvement of the working class, most especially Black workers. Sexism will not be overcome without opposing the destruction of nature by patriarchal capitalism. At various times, we may tactically focus on this or that issue, but ultimately no one oppression is morally more important than another, nor even truly separate from the others. Nor should other struggles wait until one is "solved," whether capitalism or racism or any other.

(8) The mainstream of anarchism has historically opposed capitalism in favor of a cooperative, nonprofit, self-managed, economy—that is, libertarian (or anti-authoritarian) socialism. To win this goal requires the participation of the international working class, but it also requires the participation of all oppressed people.

(9) The most revolutionary forces are likely to be found at the intersection of various oppressions—such as Black workers or working women. These are least corrupted by the relative privileges and benefits which the ruling class uses to buy off potentially rebellious people.

However, we write off no one. We appeal to both the self-interest and the potential idealism of the vast majority of humanity. For example, we call on white workers to give up their apparent, petty privileges over people of color, privileges which tie them to the ruling class. This is not so the whites will be worse off but guilt-free, but so that they will be both materially and morally better off.

(10) Oppressed people are divided by relative privileges of gender, race, class, and nationality and blinded by irrational and authoritarian beliefs. There is no pure section of society, unpoisoned by authoritarianism. Yet we have faith that people can accept human solidarity as a supreme value—that they can give up the desire to be little bosses over those even weaker than themselves, in order to reach for real freedom for themselves and all others.

(11) We want to build an organization that embodies this perspective. Anarchists are a distinct minority. Unfortunately, the vast majority of oppressed people more or less accept the system we live under. They look to leaders to save them. Anarchists hope to win over the majority by persuasion and example. As the system is

shaken by its crises, we intend to raise an alternate program to that of the authoritarians. We want to persuade people to rely on themselves by building democratic mass organizations counterpoised to the rulers and would-be new rulers. Marxists are vanguardist and authoritarian because they want to build parties that will become the new rulers. It is not vanguardist or authoritarian for the anarchist minority to persuade people of our unpopular program—that people should rely on themselves. It is part of the process of popular self-organization.

Billy and Terri (Brooklyn), Mike E. (Detroit), Kieran Frazier, Chris Hobson, Duff MacIntosh, Trip Perez, Wayne Price, Matt Quest, Tanya R., Bill Schweitzer, Ron Tabor

We welcome others to sign this statement. Please inform any current signers.

3

What We Do
BY CHRISTOPHER DAY
LOVE AND RAGE *FEDERATION BULLETIN*, APRIL 1998

INTRODUCTION

IN THIS PAPER I ATTEMPT TO STAKE OUT some of the questions that are going to confront Love and Rage after we resolve the immediate crisis precipitated by "What We Believe." I look critically at the ten-year long project of building a serious revolutionary anarchist organization and try to identify the elements in anarchist theory and our initial conception of this project that might be responsible for our failure to achieve that objective. I then argue that in order to move forward, we need to stop identifying ourselves as within the anarchist tradition but rather view ourselves as something new that takes significant things—like anti-authoritarianism and anti-statism—from anarchism. I then look at the Zapatistas as a model of an organization that was able to conceive of itself as something new, while taking things of value from older traditions that have failed. I also look at several principles of revolutionary organization that I see in the theory and practice of the EZLN. These include a level of commitment that involves being willing to make serious sacrifices, rooting ourselves in oppressed communities, and the construction of revolutionary culture. I then briefly discuss the importance of maintaining our commitment to becoming a cadre organization in opposition to the idea that we retreat to a looser network structure. Finally, I make a number of practical suggestions for things we need to do as an organization to get out of our current predicament including a collective, public self-criticism in the pages of the newspaper and organized political discussions with other groups and individuals.

THE HISTORICAL FAILURE OF LOVE AND RAGE

Ten years ago a handful of mainly young anarchist activists set out to build a serious revolutionary anarchist organization by establishing a continental anarchist newspaper. We understood that it would take time to build the kind of organization we wanted: a politically coherent and disciplined organization of organizers, what I would call a revolutionary anarchist cadre organization. We understood that there was little in the way of anarchist theory or historical practice to guide us in this project and that we would have to struggle with people against the powerful anti-organizational tendencies that exist within anarchism to make it happen. We believed that people could be won to the need for such an organization in a step-by-step fashion and that is how we proceeded. First, we won people to the value of having a continental newspaper. Then we won people to the idea of cohering the various people involved in writing, producing and distributing that newspaper into a loose network. Then we won people to the need for formalizing that network into an organization with a defined structure and politics. Then we won people to raising the expectations of membership.

After ten years of work on the project of building a revolutionary anarchist cadre organization, we still don't really have one. We have accomplished many things which we should be proud of, but we have not built the organization we set out to build. We need to honestly confront the reasons why. As I see it, there are three main ways we can explain this failure. First, we can blame the people involved and their individual failings. Second, we can blame the times and the adverse political conditions under which we have attempted to build the organization. Third and finally, we can examine the philosophical foundations of our original project.

There is enough truth in each explanation that we should take them all seriously. As the main original advocate of this project, and as a person who pushed for many of the twists and turns we have taken over the years, I feel a high level of personal responsibility for many of the errors the organization has made. I think we would all benefit from self-critically evaluating our personal roles in the successes and failures of Love and Rage. The conscious incorporation of a process of criticism and self-criticism into the political life of the organization would also do a lot to make us a healthier organization. It is also true that the period in which Love and Rage has sought to establish itself has been a bad one. Love and Rage was founded with the expectation that the 1990s would be a period of heightened activity for the social movements that most of the founding members of the project came out of. Instead, we have witnessed the almost complete decimation of the pale shadow of a radical movement that existed in the US at the end of the 1980s.

At the same time, there is a real danger that in emphasizing either of these things, we will avoid confronting some of the deeper causes of our failure. Any attempt to build a revolutionary organization must deal with the personal limitations of the people involved and errors in judgment. We are all damaged goods, products of a fucked-up society. A conception of a revolutionary organization that can't accommodate that fact and figure out how to confront it is no conception at all. Similarly, all revolutionary organizations have to figure out how to get through bad times as well as good, if they hope to succeed. On the whole, the '90s have seen the decimation of the left in the US, but some groups have adapted to the actual conditions of the times and figured out how to grow. We may not want to model ourselves directly on any one of those groups but we should seriously look into what it is about their perspectives and approaches that enabled them to thrive where everyone else has shriveled up or just hung on to what they already had. In other words, taking seriously the limitations of individuals and the nature of the period we've been in should still force us to examine the philosophical foundations of our original project.

Love and Rage is the child of a critique of Leninism and a critique of the prevailing politics of anarchism. When the people who founded Love and Rage began to coalesce as a group in the late 1980s, it was on the basis of a limited set of common notions. First, we were revolutionaries. Based on our experiences in the social movements of the 1980s or earlier, we had come to the conclusion that the changes this society needs to see can only be achieved by revolutionary means. Second, we saw the importance of building a revolutionary political organization as one part of the larger revolutionary process. Third, we rejected the two key concepts of Leninism: the vanguard party and the revolutionary state. Fourth, we identified, critically to be sure, with the revolutionary libertarian tradition in general and anarchism in particular. Fifth, we also saw ourselves as drawing insight and inspiration from anti-colonial struggles, women's liberation, queer liberation, Black liberation, and radical ecological struggles. We patched these general ideas together and called them "revolutionary anarchism." This was a term that was deliberately conceived of as enabling us to distinguish ourselves from reformist (or "evolutionary"), individualist, and anti-organizational tendencies within anarchism without aligning ourselves with any of the other already historically defined tendencies in anarchism (collectivism, anarcho-communism, syndicalism, the Platformists, etc.). We did not view any of these tendencies as offering an adequate basis for our politics and conceived of ourselves as charting our own course and redefining what anarchism meant in important ways in the process.

Underlying this whole project then, was a fundamental faith that an effective organization could redefine anarchism and give it a theoretical coherence and contemporary relevance that we all knew it didn't have in the late 1980s. WWB's attempt to inscribe in stone some sort of anarchist orthodoxy to guard against outside influences is therefore a repudiation of the spirit that originally animated Love and Rage. In many respects, Love and Rage has succeeded in redefining anarchism in the US— at the very least, by carving out more space for ideas that were previously very marginal within the anarchist movement. This is clearest on the question of race. Love and Rage aggressively challenged the prevailing class reductionism and liberalism in the anarchist movement on the question of race in US society and completely shifted the center of debate on questions of race to the point that people entering the anarchist movement in 1998 take for granted a whole series of things about the existence of and the nature of white supremacy in the US that were quite literally the views of only a handful of people in the anarchist movement in 1988. It would be possible to point to a number of other issues on which Love and Rage has dramatically shifted the terms of debate within anarchism, and we should be proud of these accomplishments. But for every point on which we have had such success, there is another on which not only have we not made headway with the rest of the anarchist movement but where we have been bogged down by our anarchism.

The areas where we have had the most success in reshaping anarchism have been largely limited to the critique of this society. This has been a historical strength of anarchism—its ability to a) adopt critiques of various features of this society from sources outside of anarchism and b) integrate them into a larger anti-authoritarian framework. From Bakunin's embrace of Marx's critique of capitalism to the willingness of many anarchists today to integrate an analysis of white skin privilege into their politics, the search for a deeper and more radical analysis of the existing society has been a hallmark of anarchism. This is in keeping with the deeply moral character of anarchism. Where anarchism has not been able to integrate ideas from outside the tradition has been precisely on questions of organizational methods, strategy, and tactics—on a positive program or plan of action for getting from this society to where we want to go. And it has been on these sorts of questions that Love and Rage has completely failed to redefine anarchism. Instead we have had to fight tooth and nail just to establish on paper the most elementary organizational norms which have in practice been largely ignored.

The question that confronts us is not whether it might be possible to develop a serious and coherent organizational theory and practice while remaining within the anarchist idiom. I think it is possible. While there are only a few of them, and while none of them achieved lasting success, there are some historical examples of revolutionary anarchist cadre organizations: the PLM in Mexico, the Platformists, to some extent the FAI, and even more the Friends of Durruti in Spain. One can patch together some lessons and analyses of these experiences and say one has an anarchist theory of revolutionary organization. But the question is: Is this the best way to construct a theory that speaks to our needs on the eve of the 21st century? What the WWB doc-

ument has made clear to me is that by defining ourselves as an organization within
anarchism, rather than as an organization that takes significant things from anarchism, we have found ourselves constantly having to re-argue the most elementary
questions of organization. By defining ourselves as within anarchism we sabotage any
serious study of the positive as well as the negative lessons of revolutionary experiences outside of anarchism (which means the vast majority of the revolutionary experiences of the 20th century).

  Love and Rage has always occupied a somewhat heretical place in the anarchist movement. We discuss issues that other anarchists ignore and we take positions
that other anarchists view as beyond the pale. If we have succeeded in redefining anarchism in the US on certain questions the inherent contradiction in our project is
probably most clearly reflected in the absence of any similar project that defines itself
as anarchist outside of North America.

No More Tradition's Chains Shall Bind Us

I want to be part of a serious and effective revolutionary organization that is committed to an anti-authoritarian vision of the new society we are fighting for, and that
clearly understands the historical failure of "state socialism" in its myriad forms in the
20th century. For ten years, we have sought to build such an organization and have
defined that project within the anarchist tradition. It seems clear to me now that we
overestimated our ability to redefine that tradition and underestimated the amount of
baggage that comes with it. At the same time, I think the anarchist critiques of other
traditions (particularly Leninism) remain fundamentally correct, and I have no interest in embracing any other existing historical trend. Basically, I think all existing revolutionary theory is out of touch with the world we live in. This has to do both with
weaknesses in the theory that have been there from the start, as well as important
changes in the world itself that the theory has failed to keep up with.

  The role of the dead weight of orthodoxy in the recent debates in Love and
Rage convinces me that we have to make some sort of radical break with how we've
conceived ourselves. The last thing we or the embryonic revolutionary movement of
the 21st century needs now is a dose of that "ol' time" anything, whether it is anarchism, Leninism, Presbyterianism, or whatever. We need fresh blood, not formalde-
hyde, coursing through our veins. If there is going to be a coherent anti-authoritarian
revolutionary theory and practice in the coming period, it must be made anew by
people participating in real social struggles on the new terrain of the post-colonial,
post-industrial, post-modern, Post Raisin Bran world we actually live in.

  I believe that the Zapatistas currently represent the most significant attempt
to construct a new revolutionary politics that sums up the failures of the past century and moves on. I don't think the Zapatistas have all the answers and, to their credit,
neither do they. Confronted with the historical failure of the old formulas of the left,
they were willing to break new ground. That didn't mean that they lost contact with
the things that had originally animated them or the historical traditions from which
they came (Marxism-Leninism, traditions of indigenous autonomy and resistance, the
Mexican Revolution, etc.) but rather that the content of those traditions would have
to be transformed in light of new conditions if it was to remain of any value. The
EZLN was founded by a dozen members of one of the many guerrilla groups that
sprung up in Mexico in the late '60s and early '70s that mainly took their inspiration

from Che Guevara and the Cuban Revolution. They found themselves in a situation in which their ideology could not answer the problems of the indigenous people of Chiapas but where their increasingly desperate situation was driving them to increasingly revolutionary conclusions. Not knowing exactly where it would lead them, the Zapatistas decided to put their faith in the struggles of the people rather than in the pre-fabricated ideology they had brought with them to the jungle. While they have rejected both the pursuit of state power and the idea of the vanguard party, the Zapatistas did not choose to define themselves as anarchists (even though anarchism has a much richer history in Mexico than in the US).

Without falling into the trap of blindly aping the Zapatistas, I think we should take a similar attitude towards our own project. Anarchism has a different complex of strengths and weaknesses than the Guevarism of the founders of the EZLN. But in the broadest sense, there is an important similarity—both ideologies are largely the products of an earlier period and both have failed to recapture the imagination of new generations because they are inadequate for new circumstances. If anything, these features are more pronounced in anarchism. The point is not to opportunistically abandon everything we have stood for in the hope of latching onto something more popular, the point is that it is only in the actual lives and struggles of the people themselves, under new conditions, that we can hope to find the answers to the problems that established ideologies have proven unable to answer. If we want to develop a coherent revolutionary politics that speaks to those new conditions we can't chain them to a political tradition that has effectively been in a coma for half a century.

Based on our experiences as an organization over the past ten years and on our knowledge of the historical accomplishments of the anarchist movement around the world since the Second World War, on what foundation can we base the hope that a significant number of people in the US, let alone the millions of people it will actually take to win, are going to be won to a revolutionary politics that calls itself anarchist? I would suggest that there is exactly no evidence to support this hope and that it is, for all intents and purposes, an act of religious faith. I'll go even further. Revolutions are life and death struggles. People are right not to put their life on the line in the name of an ideology that can't answer some of the most basic questions that people know they will face in such a struggle.

I believe that Love and Rage should be a revolutionary cadre organization that remains committed to a fundamentally libertarian perspective without narrowly defining itself within the anarchist tradition. It should be an organization that is theoretically open and flexible enough to take the lessons there are to be learned from other traditions and, more importantly, to develop new theory and practice in response to new conditions. For the moment, the best model of such an organization we have is the Zapatistas and I think we should look much more closely at their experience to see what it has to teach us. (I've been reading a lot about the Zapatistas but most of the information I use here can be found in *El Sueño Zapatista* and *La Rebelion de las Cañadas*.)

SOME LESSONS OF ZAPATISMO

I would suggest that there are a handful of basic principles that can be derived from what we know about the history and development of the Zapatistas. Some of these are particular to the Zapatistas in that they are advances on the theory and practice of other revolutionary trends. Others are elementary lessons that have been learned over and over again by every even moderately successful revolutionary movement.

The first principle is that to be a revolutionary and to build a revolutionary organization can not be a hobby or a part-time thing. All of the conditions for building a revolutionary movement in the mountains and jungles of Chiapas existed in the 1980s, but the struggle would never have gone beyond the interminable fights over this and that piece of land that had been going on for decades and centuries if a hard core of a dozen determined individuals hadn't decided to give up everything in order to found the EZLN in a remote corner of the Lacandon Jungle in 1983. The hard core must have some common politics but much more important than total ideological uniformity is a commitment to collective participation in the struggle. The founding members of the EZLN included people with a variety of political backgrounds: Guevarists from the armed organizations of the 1970s, veterans of Maoist initiated campesino organizations, catechists versed in liberation theology, and those who identified primarily with the long traditions of indigenous resistance to the European conquest. What united them was a high level of commitment to a common project—building the EZLN—and an acknowledgment that not one of them had all the answers and that they would have to learn from each other and from the process of carrying out their work collectively.

A second principle that the experience of the Zapatistas has to teach us is the central importance of rooting ourselves among the oppressed. For the middle-class members of the group that founded the EZLN, this meant patiently winning the trust of the people, learning their languages and customs, placing real faith in the people, and not pretending to know what was best for them. It also meant giving up undoubtedly promising professional careers in academia and medicine and elsewhere in order to spend long years going hungry, getting sick, being bitten by bugs, and feeling completely cut off from the comforts and pleasures of the life they had left behind. It meant immersing themselves in the lives of largely illiterate peasants.

A genuine revolutionary organization must be an organization of people who live, work, study, and play among the oppressed who are most likely to be won to the need for revolution. In the US, I would argue, this means poor and mainly people of color communities. For an organization like Love and Rage that is overwhelmingly white, disproportionately middle class, and whose members are closely tied to either white youth subcultures or academia, this means some big changes. We can not hope to really make revolution if we are not willing to live and work in the ghettos, barrios, housing projects, and poor rural communities of the US. People are going to be understandably reluctant to make those kinds of changes without some assurance that others are doing it with them, and that assurance can only come from a group that has the high level of commitment to a collectively formulated common project. But no revolutionary project can promise success and that means that there must be a certain amount of individual will to do whatever it takes to build a revolutionary movement. Individually, some of us have already gone further down this road than others. But so far ALL OF US have failed to turn this into a collective process. The personal decisions we have been making about where we live, where we work, whether or not to go to college or graduate school, have all had political consequences for the organization but have all been made as personal decisions without even a shred of collective accountability to the people we are working with. This individualist approach reinforces existing class inequalities in the organization and turns what should be political discussions of where we live and work into moralistic arguments. The result of this is that collective bonds that are needed to hold a revolutionary organization together are corroded and theoretical rigor and coherence are sacrificed on the altar of an anti-intellectual caricature of the working class.

REVOLUTIONARY CULTURE

Finally, I want to mention the importance of culture in the success of the Zapatistas. The founders of the EZLN understood the importance both of respecting the traditions and customs of the communities they were seeking to root themselves in and of creating a new revolutionary culture. A revolutionary movement cannot simply be built around a political line. It is not sufficient to have the correct analysis of imperialism or the class struggle or whatever. A revolutionary movement stands in a particular relationship to the culture of the people it seeks to organize. A revolutionary movement that doesn't sing, dance, eat, and write poetry with the people cannot hope to win them to revolutionary politics. But beyond this purely instrumental view of culture, a revolutionary movement that is not immersed in the culture of the people cannot hope to understand their actual conditions and what it will take to win. Culture is a vehicle for the accumulated experiences of a people. Subcommandante Marcos talks about the importance for the EZLN, not just in learning how to speak the languages of the indigenous peoples, but in learning their folk tales and what they symbolized and how in this process of translation, their politics were transformed and given new meaning. At the same time that the culture of the indigenous communities was transforming the politics of the EZLN, they were transforming the culture of those communities by introducing new practices and customs, revolutionary songs and celebrations that injected new ideas and values into the lives of the people. In other words, it is not sufficient to just adopt the culture of the people as if it is in itself revolutionary. It is necessary to draw out the revolutionary aspects, to strengthen them, and to consciously create a revolutionary culture.

Love and Rage is culturally tied to the white middle-class and academic origins of most of its membership. It is a culture that values rigorous and rational argument (which is good) but that puts little value on the things that actually hold communities together. So we are really good at arguing with each other but really bad at doing the things that express our love for each other and that remind us that we have to hang together. It should hardly be a surprise then, that we have such difficulties holding our organization together let alone broadening its appeal. If we are going to immerse ourselves in oppressed communities, we need to commit ourselves to creating revolutionary culture. Every successful radical social movement in US history has done so. Whether it was the songs of the IWW or of the Civil Rights movement or the creation of new holidays like Mayday or Juneteenth, the conscious deliberate creation of a new culture (often employing many existing cultural elements) has always been present. Without such a culture as a counterweight, the often heated arguments that inevitably characterize any genuine revolutionary movement will tear the thing apart before it can even get off the ground.

THE ORGANIZATION WE NEED

It is tempting to reconsider the value of a looser, less demanding network structure in light of the difficulties involved in making Love and Rage a tighter, more disciplined organization. It probably seems to many that the only way we can hope to survive at all is by reverting to the network structure and that since we've never really been able to put into practice the vision of Love and Rage as a cadre organization, we aren't really giving up anything by abandoning that conception.

A network implies an organization that doesn't demand as high a level of theoretical unity because it isn't attempting to establish a high level of practical unity. A network implies that the primary function of the organization is to share information rather than to coordinate action, because once you try to coordinate action the theoretical differences that can coexist in a loose network become practical differences over which course of action to follow.

The idea of retreating to a network structure is based on the belief that a network can keep people in touch even if it is not currently possible to carry out coordinated activity and that the structures for such coordinated activity will emerge out of a network when they are appropriate. There are some truths in all this. Some of Love and Rage's greatest contributions to the movement have been carrying out precisely these sorts of network functions by publishing the newspaper, organizing conferences, maintaining the listserv, and publishing the *Fed Bull*. These are all things that need to continue. But the idea of a cadre organization is not hostile to these things. On the contrary, it says that the network functions will be carried out more consistently and that the contacts between people that are maintained by these functions will be stronger if there is an organization of the most serious and dedicated activists committed to doing that work. The history of the anarchist movement in the US is littered with networks and federations that have come and gone precisely because they did not understand this elementary fact.

If Love and Rage is to survive and flourish, it must become a cadre organization even if that means we end up being only a few dozen strong. This does not mean we should become a sect nor that we should cut off the relations we have with people who can't or don't want to be in a cadre organization. On the contrary, by making a clearer distinction between those who have committed themselves to the work of building Love and Rage and those who are sympathetic with our political outlook, we enable ourselves to relate to those people in a more principled way and to carry out the work of expanding the network that exists around the organization by doing our work more consistently, more deliberately, and more strategically.

TO RISE ON NEW FOUNDATIONS

So far, I have argued for certain general principles that I think need to inform Love and Rage's future work. The current crisis in Love and Rage means we cannot continue functioning as we have in the past, that we need to make a radical break and reconceive our project. But what does this mean concretely? We should not imagine that there is some sort of quick fix that can make Love and Rage the organization we want it to be overnight. We need to be much more serious about the collective development of both our theory and practice. This will take time. But there are several things we can do now.

One, we need to carry out a collective and public self-criticism in which we analyze our history as an organization, acknowledge our errors, and attempt to identify why they happened. The special issue of *Class War* that appeared last summer is a good model for the kind of thing we need to do. There are two reasons to do this. First, it is important to clarify these things for ourselves so that we can move forward without repeating the same mistakes or feeling responsible for defending things we did that were mistaken. Second, it is an important step in initiating discussions with groups and individuals outside Love and Rage. It enables us to acknowledge specific criticisms others may have of us and, more importantly, establishes that we are open to hearing criticism.

Two, we need to initiate organized political discussions broadly with the various groups and individuals we work with and respect. The membership of Love and Rage alone is too narrow a group for us to satisfactorily carry out the important discussions that have emerged within the organization. This needs to happen on all levels. We need to use the newspaper to draw people from outside of the organization into these discussions. We need to use conferences and other public events. And we need to sit down face-to-face with other groups. There are two main reasons to do this. First, there are too damn few of us and we need to cast our nets wider if we want to be part of a broader revolutionary movement and not just an isolated sect. Second, organized political discussion will force us to clarify our own politics in a way that we have manifestly failed to do in the past ten years. There are a lot of groups and individuals we should be talking to. There are other explicitly anarchist formations like the Anarchist Communist Federation and the ABC-Federation. There are a number of revolutionary collectives that include anarchists like Fireworks in the Bay Area and R'n'B in Brooklyn. There are collectives like STORM and FIST that don't include anarchists but that seem to be oriented towards developing a new revolutionary politics. There are the various non-sectarian (though often reformist) Marxist groups that have opened up to criticism in response to the "crisis in socialism" like Freedom Road, Solidarity, and even the Committees of Correspondence. I would expect discussions with different groups to fulfill different functions for us—in some cases opening the way for closer collaboration and in others clarifying our differences. The important thing is that we understand the value in both developments and that we have things to learn from everybody even if we find we have fundamental philosophical differences.

Three, we need to be engaged in organized collective study and discussion. The New York local has begun to meet again to study and discuss the political questions that have been raised by the current crisis in the organization. But we need to be engaged in this kind of study and discussion across the organization so that we don't talk past each other when we use terms and references that have different meanings for different people or that just aren't understood. The *Fed Bull* should become a vehicle for Federation-wide collective study and the Coordinating Committee (CC) should be delegated to develop a study program to appear in installments in the *Fed Bull* to broaden the base of common knowledge of revolutionary theory and history within the organization.

Four, everybody in the organization should write a thorough political report on the work they are doing. The most important thing that Love and Rage has is a few dozen good activists. This is not always apparent because a lot of the activism that Love and Rage members are engaged in never gets reported either in the pages of the newspaper nor in reports to the *Fed Bull*. One only finds out about it if one is able to talk with lots of members one-on-one. Yet the fact remains that Love and Rage members are active participants in a wide range of social struggles in three countries. There are Love and Rage members involved in workplace struggles among university adjuncts, at UPS, and in organizing service workers. One Love and Rage member is involved in a workplace safety struggle involving Black women workers who are routinely exposed to dangerous chemicals on the factory floor. There are Love and Rage members involved in the defense of old growth forests. Several Love and Rage members are involved in Zapatista solidarity work in several cities. One Love and Rage member is interning at the Puerto Rican Cultural Center. Another is organizing to throw the DARE program out of the school she teaches at. Love and Rage members are involved in an ongoing way in the fight to free Mumia and in organizing for the Jericho '98 March on Washington. Love and Rage members are involved in welfare rights struggles in three different states. There is one Love and Rage member active in anti-police brutality work. Several members are working in Anti-Racist Action. Love and Rage members continue to play an important role in the struggles at CUNY in defense of open admissions. Two Love and Rage members are working on organizing a winter seminar on revolutionary theory. Two local groups have study groups going.

If the few dozen activists who are keeping Love and Rage alive were each to write a thorough, reflective, critical report on the work they've been doing, the problems they've encountered, and the lessons they've drawn from those experiences the whole character of the organization would change. Debates that seem stupid or overly abstract that have dominated some recent discussions would be drowned in a discussion of our real problems. The false but demoralizing sense that nobody is doing anything real would evaporate. This is not to say that some of the questions that currently divide the organization would disappear but rather that they would be cast in a whole new light and their practical importance in our actual work would be much clearer than is currently the case. By a political report I don't mean just an account of all the meetings and demonstrations a person has attended, but rather an attempt to critically analyze the work for the benefit of the whole organization. The theoretical issues that really matter would push aside those that don't.

All of these suggestions are focused in some sense on the development of our politics and yet none of them are suggestions directed at our mass work. This is not because I don't see that as important. Obviously I do. I believe that we need to be engaged in some sort of common mass work, if only some sort of campaign that we can carry out in the different places where we are already working. I think we also need to be discussing much more seriously what it means to truly root ourselves in oppressed communities and take some collective steps in that direction. But both of these things must come out of the sort of collective process of reassessing our politics that I've described above. We can't seriously discuss where we need to go if we don't know where we are and where we've been. The process of collective self-criticism is about figuring out where we've been and the process of writing thorough individual political reports is about determining where we actually are right now.

CONCLUSION

In this paper I've tried to raise a number of the deeper issues that I think underlie the current crisis in Love and Rage beyond the immediate questions raised by "What We Believe." I've put forward some principles of revolutionary organization that I've seen modeled by the Zapatistas and some concrete suggestions for rectifying some of the weaknesses of our own organization. I intend to flesh some of these ideas out into more concrete proposals before the upcoming conference, but I'm eager to know what people think of the ideas put forward here before I do so. I've found the current crisis in Love and Rage personally painful and profoundly challenging to some of my longest held convictions. But none of this has shaken my commitment to building a serious anti-authoritarian revolutionary organization no matter what it takes.

4

Struggle on Three Fronts

By Joel Olson
Love and Rage *Federation Bulletin*, May 1998

THE CURRENT SPLIT IN LOVE AND RAGE has so far appeared as a struggle between two hostile camps, the "What We Believe" side and the anti-WWB side. (Although the majority position is probably in the "Who Cares I'm Outta Here" camp.) I believe it is a serious error to think of the present split strictly in terms of pro- and anti-WWB. Instead, the debate needs to focus on the key political issues that people are struggling over. While there is no hope whatsoever of saving Love and Rage, for those of us who remain committed to the idea of building a strong revolutionary organization (I do not consider the suggestion to go back to a network to be a serious one), we need to hash out our individual positions on these key issues and then see if we can build new political formations based on shared politics.

Other people have recognized the need for us to move forward after the conference. However, the biggest problem with the proposals for a new organization, whether it's a revised Love and Rage (see Suzy and James's "Proposal for a New Love and Rage" as well as Laura's "Draft Resolution on Membership" in the April, 1998 *Fed Bull*) or a post-Love and Rage organization (see Chris's proposal in this issue as well as Brad's writings on cadre organization in the April, 1998 *Fed Bull*) exclusively focus on the structural problems of Love and Rage and do not address the political problems. This is exactly backwards. While I support the move of any anti-authoritarian revolutionary organization toward a tighter, cadre-type organization that is both more effective and accountable than Love and Rage's current structure, the heart of the split is over politics, and that's what we need to keep front and center.

There are three key political issues at stake, in my opinion. These three issues are anti-statism, a correct analysis of white supremacy, and the need to commit ourselves to dual power strategies in choosing and developing political projects. In the rest of this article I want to explain these three positions, the debates as they've been played out so far, and what I think is the best position on each. My vision of a new revolutionary organization should be clear from the positions I take on these three issues.

I. ANTI-STATISM: THE CORE OF ANTI-AUTHORITARIANISM

The center of the debate over building a "multi-tendency" organization is not about the ideological beliefs of imaginary members who might or might not join Love and Rage in the future. Rather, it is about existing members' definition of anti-authoritarianism. For my part, the key elements that define anti-authoritarianism are a) a belief in the relative autonomy of oppressions (i.e. there is no one form of oppression, like class or social hierarchy, that all other forms "really" boil down to), b) opposition to vanguardism and support for directly democratic models of political organization, c) a belief in the self activity of the masses, and d) opposition to the state, either as an "intermediate" stage in the struggle for a classless society or as the permanent political form of the new society. To me anti-statism must be a core element of any definition of anti-authoritarianism.

Anti-statism is at the center of this dispute: WWBers rightly insist on it as the core of anti-authoritarian politics, while Brad and Carolyn have been mum on whether anti-statism is a part of their definition of "anti-authoritarian." (Chris and Jessica have been explicit in their anti-statism, but no one who signed WWB will believe them. I do believe them.) But instead of seriously debating this question, we get arrogant assertions of the superiority of "old time anarchism" from WWBers and equally dogmatic assertions of the superiority of Marxism from Brad ("Anarchism, Marxism, and Love and Rage," April 1998, *Federation Bulletin*). WWB essentially amounts to an anarchist loyalty oath: anarchism is the truth at its core, Marxism is authoritarian at its core, therefore all persons in Love and Rage must pledge allegiance to anarchy and shake their fists at any hints of creeping Marxism. But Brad's supposed defense of the "multi-tendency" position just flips the good guys and bad guys around: now it's Marxism which is the only element of Love and Rage that has been structured, coherent, organized, and effective, while anarchism has been nothing but flaky, ineffective, and bourgeois.

The only way out of this mess is to completely reject the dichotomy that WWB establishes (anarchy good, Marxism bad) and that Brad ultimately shares (Marxism good, anarchy bad). The way out is to focus on the real issue at hand, the differing conceptions of anti-authoritarianism and the role of the state in each. The WWB signers are correct to point out that the critique of the state is traditionally an anarchist tenet (though anarchists have no monopoly on critiques of the state). They are also right to point out that Brad and Carolyn have conspicuously evaded the question of anti-statism. I agree with them that our opposition to the state must be unambiguous and that it is reasonable and appropriate to challenge comrades who in some way feel that a state is part of the long term revolutionary struggle.

But it is wrong to make this a dividing line issue when a full debate has not even begun on the question. WWB emerged in the context of a broiling split within the New York local. Those of us not in New York, however, didn't have a fucking clue what was going on there. Some of us knew there were problems but few of us outsiders knew the political differences at hand because no one in New York reported them in the *Fed Bull*. So, when WWB did come out it was an unexpected bombshell. The consequence, intended or not, was to cut off debate on the question of anti-authoritarianism and to make it a "dividing line question" without a full and free debate beforehand. Thus, what WWB amounted to for many of us was a loyalty oath, not an invitation to debate.

What a revolutionary organization needs, then, is not a pledge to anarchy nor a watered-down definition of "anti-authoritarianism" but a collective agreement about the content of anti-authoritarianism. This content, I maintain, must contain the elements I outlined above (though my definition is probably not exhaustive). In particular, it means a resolute opposition to the state and an agreement that any activism we engage in will work to weaken state power. Once we have that, whether one comes to such politics through anarchism, council communism, indigenism, anti-imperialism, or a creative interpretation of Star Trek's Prime Directive is irrelevant. These politics imply a "multi-tendency" organization in the sense of bringing together multiple ideologies and orientations all unified by a common definition of authoritarianism and an agreement that it has nothing to do with freedom.

II. A CORRECT ANALYSIS OF WHITE SUPREMACY

Wayne thinks that questions of race are "negotiable" (see "What We Think" in this *Fed Bull*). I disagree. A revolutionary organization in the US absolutely needs unity on two matters relating to race. First, its members must agree on a political analysis that places white supremacy at the center of American history. Second, members must agree that developing strategies to fight white supremacy must be at the heart of all our key political work. Agreement on these two principles is not, in my mind, negotiable. Instead, they form the basis of the politics of the organization I want to help build after Love and Rage. Wayne disagrees on both counts. He does not believe that an analysis of white supremacy should be at the center of our politics beyond a general critique of "authoritarianism," of which racism is one form. As a consequence, he sees no compelling need to make the struggle against white supremacy central to our activism. I'm sure he'd be happy if someone took the work on, but it's one sphere of struggle among many, which members may or may not choose to focus on.

My general position on white supremacy is spelled out in the "Draft Resolution [on White Supremacy]" published in the last *Fed Bull*, so I won't repeat it here. However, I want to respond to recent criticisms of my position on white supremacy by Wayne ("What We Think Are the Issues," this *Fed Bull*) and Bill Meyers ("Multi-racial Muddling," April 1998 *Fed Bull*). Both Wayne and Bill are intelligent people, so I cannot believe that they have grossly misrepresented my (and others') analysis of white skin privilege because they don't understand it. I must assume that they deliberately choose to distort and disregard the analysis of white privilege because it challenges their essentially class-reductionist position that divisions among the working class ain't all that strong and that racism, however evil, is a secondary issue in the broad scheme of things.

For example, Bill claims that the theory of white skin privilege is aimed only at white people. This is flat-out wrong. If anything, it's people of color who have done the bulk of the work analyzing the system of white privilege and agitating against it. White folks are the newcomers. As numerous people from Sojourner Truth to W.E.B. Du Bois to Malcolm X have pointed out, the struggle against white supremacy is the central task facing all Americans, of whatever race.

For his part, Wayne claims that I argue that white workers are better off because of racism and that I imply that fascism would be good for the white working class. I have never argued either position. That Wayne chooses to grossly, almost hilariously—"Racists say that your [white workers'] interests are against Black people, and… [the "Draft Resolution" signers] do too")—distort the theory of white skin privilege is a result of ideological blinders that he puts on himself.

There are two ways to refer to white privileges as "petty." On the one hand, when compared to a truly free world, having first crack at the best jobs (all of which stink), being last hired and first fired (for a shitty job), living in the better neighborhoods (most of which are still no good), giving one's kids the best public education (so they can be well-paid worker drones when they grow up, too), etc. are "petty" indeed. No privilege held can compare to a world in which privilege does not exist. I think Wayne and I agree on this point. On the other hand, however, to call white privileges "petty" is also a way to dismiss the role of white supremacy in the construction of our unfreedom as relatively unimportant. From what Wayne has written, I believe he considers the wages of whiteness to be "petty" in this sense too, and here I could not disagree more. White supremacy has been absolutely crucial in the construction and development of every major political, economic, and social institution in this country, from the creation of the two-party system to the weakness of labor unions to the impoverishment of the South to popular attitudes toward birth control to women's liberation to the length of the working day to the songs we listen to on the radio.

White unanimity is both the secret to American capitalism's success and its weak link. Smashing white supremacy will not mean that all other forms of oppression will magically disappear afterward, not at all. However, history shows that the struggle against white supremacy also creates political space to challenge other forms of oppression from a position of strength. It creates situations and possibilities to build new social relationships and institutions that we can only dream of now. There is nothing "petty" or "stagist" or "reductionist" about this analysis of history. It is the cornerstone of revolutionary work.

One other point: when the "Draft Resolution" reads that the struggle against white supremacy "will mean a quantitative reduction in the standard of living for many workers in imperialist countries in general and for white workers in the US in particular," it doesn't mean that we have to tell poor workers to embrace their poverty or to try to "win over" better-off workers by threatening to take what they have. It simply means that the world cannot support six billion people with two cars and 300 channels. Revolutionaries who try to win people over with such promises a) are liars and b) treat freedom like a commodity more than the bourgeoisie does. People have to be won over to a vision of a completely new world in which one's "standard of living" is judged by the creative control they have over their own lives, not by how much stuff they have. The struggle against white supremacy is a struggle against this impoverished conception of freedom. If the language of the resolution does not reflect that then the language should be changed, but the political point still stands.

Unfortunately, however, it's not just Wayne and Bill who don't take the criticism of this second notion of "petty privileges" to heart. Many members who probably oppose most of WWB also consider "doing anti-racist" work as one choice among a variety of types of activism we could be doing. But this viewpoint of "relatively autonomous forms of oppression, relatively autonomous struggles against them, so pick and choose which oppression you want to fight" ignores how, in the United States, white supremacy structures the way all forms of oppressions—even though they are all relatively autonomous—operate and the way in which various factions struggle around them. What we need to do is figure out how racial privilege is at work in these "other" struggles—even if they usually go under the name of union organizing, reproductive freedom, rent control, tuition hikes, school financing, welfare organizing, or community policing—and figure out ways to attack it, recognizing that smashing white privilege is a necessary prerequisite of not just winning that particular struggle but clearing the way for a more radical struggle.

As an example, let's take the work the Vermont local is doing around the Living Wage Campaign, union issues, and other "class issues." To begin, with I want to say that, from the reports they submit to the *Fed Bull* and the articles they write for the newspaper, I think the work they did for the livable wage campaign was incredible. The door-to-door work, the coalition building, the strategizing—all of it seems to me to epitomize effective, influential political work with a radical bent that is done in a directly democratic manner. They have certainly gone far beyond any successes I can claim with my own activism. Nevertheless, several things about their work troubles me. At the Lansing conference, Jason reported that because Vermont was 98% white, race wasn't really a good issue to organize around there, so instead they decided to focus on "class issues." Now, without accusing the #10 folks of racism or anything like that, it seems that what focusing on "class issues" really comes to mean in this context is focusing on the white working class. This wouldn't necessarily be a problem if the aim of the work was to get white workers to recognize that the struggle to uplift workers of color is a struggle to uplift whites as well, even if it undercuts some of their "petty privileges" (here the term is appropriate). But the struggle for a livable wage, as good as it is, doesn't do that. Sure, it raises the minimum wage of all workers regardless of race, in that sense it is a progressive measure that we should all cheer. But when Black unemployment levels are historically always double that of whites in the US, how does raising the minimum wage unify the working class when Black workers won't be able to enjoy it because they can't get jobs? If white workers actively or passively defend this disparity in unemployment rates, we still have a breach in the class. Thus, the prospects for radical political movement in such a campaign hit a white wall. To repeat, a livable wage is a progressive measure that we should all support, but because it leaves white privilege intact it cannot, I believe, ultimately provide the basis to create a unified working class, which is the prerequisite for more radical struggles, such as the abolition of wage labor itself. Thus, the most such a campaign can do is win social democratic reforms, educate radicals for later struggles, and (hopefully) radicalize folks who previously weren't active. I do not want to dismiss these benefits at all; they are important. But by themselves they cannot threaten official society. That requires a campaign that gets to the heart of what keeps capitalism functioning, and that heart, in the United States at least, is the wages of whiteness.

I use the Vermonters as an example because their work has generally been so successful, not because they are any more chauvinist or shortsighted than the rest of us. (I also apologize to the #10 folks for not raising this issue with them right after Lansing as I intended.) The Vermont local is by no means the only crew to make this mistake. By and large, I think the entire anti-austerity working group has worked according to the same incorrect logic. The editors of *Race Traitor* made a similar critique of this logic in their critique of the CUNY work by the New York local (See the Aug./Sept. 1997 *Love and Rage*). Unfortunately, New Yorkers responded defensively and dismissively rather than seriously considering the critique. Such defensiveness is understandable when you've poured your soul into a struggle only to have it challenged at its core, but it's unfortunate when that defensiveness refuses to give way to self-criticism, especially when the defensiveness is expressed publicly in the newspaper.

Placing white supremacy at the core of our activism won't necessarily make activism any easier. The Vermont folks are right: it is tough to get an angle on how to fight white supremacy in a state that is 98% white. However, this doesn't mean we abandon our analysis of American history. (After all, there are reasons why Vermont, one of the few states that allowed Black suffrage in the pre-Civil War era, is 98% white—white folks did all they could to prevent free Black persons and fugitive slaves from settling there.) It means we have to be innovative in figuring out how to apply it. It might mean that struggles that are currently "popular" or attract more people (to the extent that any left wing struggle is popular in the 1990s) might not be the best ones for us to engage in. But if our analysis is right, twelve people can do more damage in a crucially strategic campaign than 1200 in campaign with politics that limit it to social democratic outcomes. It might mean we have to abandon some struggles or radically alter their aims and tactics. But that shouldn't be too big a problem because we're committed to freedom, not issues.

Wayne contends that the question of white privilege is only being raised to distract people from "the Stalinist issue." I can't speak for anyone else, but I have been raising this question well before WWB, and I ain't hiding no Stalin statue in my coat anyway. In my opinion, the politics of the "Draft Resolution on White Supremacy," whatever its wording problems (hey, it's a draft resolution) isn't "negotiable." It is a dividing line issue. I have no desire to be in a group that doesn't take these politics to heart, because I know it will be an organization destined to failure. It may be an efficient, disciplined organization that wins reforms and manages to build a modest membership, but it will pose no revolutionary threat to the powers that be.

III. A COMMITMENT TO DUAL POWER STRATEGIES

I keep pushing the white privilege analysis for two reasons. First, a free society has no room for racial discrimination or the system of "race" as we know it, so it must be smashed. It is evil and keeps all of us, regardless of skin color, from being free. But second, I am convinced that the struggle against white supremacy has the best chance of creating a situation of dual power in the US. While I do not believe racism is the "primary" form of oppression that, once conquered, will magically eliminate all other forms of oppression in its wake (which is what many socialists believe of class), I do believe that the peculiar history of the United States and its systems of racial slavery, Jim Crow, and white democracy means that white supremacy is the cotter pin that holds American capitalist society together, and that in the process of removing that pin we clear the table for a struggle against all forms of oppression, and clearing the table can begin the process of building a totally new society.

I've discussed dual power numerous times in the *Fed Bull* so I'll simply restate my definition here: an action or campaign that directly challenges the existing institutions of power in this world and—even if in just some small way—prefigures the new society we want to build. Chris's excellent article, "Dual Power in the Selva Lacondon" on dual power and the Zapatistas fleshes out this definition in a much better way than I ever have, so I'll refer the reader to that article for more explanation.

As Chris argues, a situation of dual power is like the Zapatistas setting up parallel administrations in forty "liberated zones" throughout Chiapas, but it also has relevance to the mundane and much less exciting activism we are all engaged in. Doing activism is vital but it isn't enough. What we as revolutionaries must constantly ask ourselves is, what is the content of our activism? What implications does it or could it have on the society at large? Does it challenge the powers that be or does it in some way, consciously or unconsciously, end up strengthening the hand of one of our enemies, whether it's the state, the right, or the "progressive" but essentially bourgeois left? I am not saying that fighting for reforms is inherently reactionary or bourgeois— not at all. What I am saying is that the reforms we do win should weaken the power of official society rather than strengthen it.

For example, pro-choice groups recently celebrated the lawsuit they won against radical anti-choice groups based on RICO, a set of laws that were originally established to use against the Mafia. But by using these laws, the pro-choice groups have strengthened the hand of the state at the same time that they've weakened the right. What they've essentially done is given the state another weapon they can use against both the left and the right in their quest to ensure the peaceable and steady accumulation of capital. As revolutionaries, we never want to make the mistake these progressives made in using RICO, even if it makes our struggle against the right more difficult.

A dual power strategy is about building campaigns that no institution of official society—whether it be the state, capital, conservatives, or liberals—can seize upon and steer toward their ends. In so doing, we not only destabilize official society, we show that the self-activity of the working class is the seed from which a truly free society will grow and flower. Unfortunately, such thinking does not seem to guide our activism. Instead, we have tended to choose our activism based on what many of us are already doing (such as prison and Zapatista and antifascist work in '95) or by what seems to be "hot" issues nationally (such as "anti-austerity" work in '97).

One result of this is that the debate over activist strategy surrounding WWB has focused on a false dichotomy between the "mass line" strategy versus the "just equals" strategy. The debate between these two positions is partly over how we as activists relate to the masses of "ordinary" people (i.e. non-revolutionaries). On this question I think it is obvious that whatever our organizational or leadership skills (such as they are), we are of the masses and not apart from them and should look at everything from that perspective. I don't think anyone even disagrees with that. But the debate is also about how to build a revolutionary organization, and on this question both sides are wrong. Each, in their own way, skirts around the real question of activism: how to build an anti-authoritarian dual power that has the potential to build a classless, stateless society.

For an example of the mass line side's errors, take Carolyn's articles "Road to Nowhere" and "Strategy Without Teeth" in the last two *Fed Bulls*. Carolyn argues that the revolutionary task is to figure out which reforms can be extracted from the system, to fight to win them (acting in tandem with reformist groups such as unions and liberals when appropriate), and to link reform struggles to a broader revolutionary strategy. The mass line perspective says we should determine our position on various struggles (strikes, student movements, national liberation struggles, etc.) based on the desires of "the majority" of the masses involved in the struggles. In other words, how we intervene in such struggles should be based on our assessment of what the masses want. But revolutionary politics are by definition minority politics. The revolutionary is in the minority until the barricades go up, the police attack, and the people who had been "neutral" choose to fight for the new society rather than cling to the old one. When one organizes based on what the majority "wants," what one generally ends up doing is supporting "the politics of the possible." Hence Mike E's criticism that the end result of such a strategy is social democratic liberalism is on point here. In that what we revolutionaries want is something much more, it is also (potentially, at least) deceptive to work on behalf of the "majority position" in order to undermine it. Hence Kieran's criticism that mass line is manipulative is on point as well.

You might also notice that the content of the revolutionary struggle is something Carolyn's articles hardly touch on, even though we all know that "revolutionary movements" often have as much to do with winning freedom as ice skates have to do with winning basketball games. To their credit, the content of the revolutionary struggle is precisely Kieran and Mike E's concern. However, their "just equals" approach suffers from other flaws. Mike and Kieran argue that we should judge all struggles according to a set of basic anarchist principles. We intervene by locating a group or tendency that most closely approximates these anarchist principles or, if none exists, we go in there and try to establish a beachhead of such principles to appeal to the "anti-authoritarian spirit" present in the peoples' hearts.

I am sympathetic to the principles Kieran and Mike use to critique popular movements. I am especially sympathetic to the "ruthless criticism of everything existing" (to steal a phrase from Marx) that such principles tend to produce: if anyone can find an authoritarian and anti-democratic streak in any movement, it's [Kieran]. But their application of these principles to every struggle is formulaic and ahistorical. Because social formations (including, alas, the Zapatistas) hardly ever fight on behalf of all the anarchist principles Kieran and Mike uphold, Kieran and Mike end up calling for the creation of such formations. Thus, the principles really offer no effective guide as to the practicalities of how to intervene in a struggle. Kieran and Mike end up with a series of platitudes about how a struggle should build "independent, direct action groups" without any meaningful suggestion how to do it, without indicating which actual players in the struggle are most likely to build them, and without any explanation for why such anti-authoritarian groups haven't been built yet—or if they have, why they're so small. The "just equals" position on strategy tends to end up, as Carolyn points out, as a moral principle simplistically applied to every situation.

Kieran argues that the anti-authoritarian spirit is within all of us. That may be true, but his organizing strategy does not explain why the "egoistic" side of human nature, as he puts it, (I personally don't believe in the anti-authoritarian/egoistic split he does, or in a "human nature," period) seems to win out over the anti-authoritarian spirit every time. Nor does he offer a way to help the anti-authoritarian spirit win next time. Without a strategy that helps us choose our struggles according to our best judgment of what has the best chance of building a democratic dual power, we're going to end up either taking the lonely moral high road, as Kieran and Mike do, or the crowded reformist low road, as Carolyn does. From a revolutionary perspective, both—to steal a line from Carolyn—are roads to nowhere.

For example, take the Palestinian struggle in Israel. Carolyn essentially argues that we should support the PLO's strategy because the majority of Palestinians do. Our task as revolutionaries, then, is to support the PLO-led peace process while trying to figure out a way to advance the revolutionary struggle further. Kieran, on the other hand, argues (correctly, in my opinion) that the PLO is really just another gang of elites setting themselves up to be the new Palestinian ruling class. Instead, he says, we should support the creation of a renewed Intifada, one that would seize upon and further develop the anti-authoritarian spirit of the 1980s uprisings. Unfortunately, as Carolyn (correctly, in my opinion) points out, there is no social force calling for, or working toward, an anti-authoritarian Intifada. The outcome of Kieran's strategy is that we either end up supporting the two anarchists in Palestine (we'll probably only support one—they've likely had a bitter split) or howling in the wind about the need for anti-authoritarian direct action groups to overthrow the Israeli and PLO oppressors.

A dual power strategy would start by asking different questions. First, it would ask what is the precondition of the end of Palestinian oppression and freedom for all Israelis whether Jewish, Palestinian or Arab? Answer: the destruction of the

Israeli state, which is essentially an apartheid state. Second, which social forces out there are calling for this? Answer: the PLO (at least they used to) and Hamas, the Islamic fundamentalist organization. Third, of these two forces, do either represent the potential to build a revolutionary dual power? Answer: not the PLO, who are setting themselves up to be the new ruling class in what will probably resemble a neo-colonial relationship between a Palestinian "statelet" and Israel, but quite possibly Hamas, who resolutely call for the destruction of Israel by any means necessary. Fourth, would a struggle initiated by Hamas against the Israeli state be a struggle for freedom? Here's where we as revolutionaries have to make some judgments. Clearly, Hamas itself is no friend of anarchism. Its vision of a just world is something all of us would oppose for one reason or another. So we have to ask ourselves, are there other tendencies within the broader movement that Hamas heads that are more politically advanced? What class base is behind Hamas? Most importantly, do any historical forces exist that would strip a revolutionary situation out of Hamas's hands and into the hands of the people, clearing the way for a broad struggle against all forms of oppression? Figuring this out, and developing programs to build such forces, would constitute a dual power strategy in Palestine.

It's similar to the Civil War in the United States. Neither the North nor the South was even for the abolition of slavery, much less for a classless society. Yet as Marx himself recognized, the key to building a unified working class then was the struggle against slavery and to recognize Black people as part of the working class. Thus, he supported the North against the South, not because he wanted to help the Northern capitalists but because he recognized that the historical forces at play would likely spin out of the Northern elite's control, creating the conditions that would not only force the North to make the war an antislavery war but that would challenge the rule of capital itself. As a result, the Civil War was one of America's golden opportunities to end racism and to potentially build a society run by the working class, only the opportunity was tragically snuffed out with the ending of Reconstruction. (This argument is spelled out beautifully in Du Bois's *Black Reconstruction*, if you're interested.)

Now, let's apply this to our own situation. What are the preconditions for an anti-authoritarian revolution in the United States? A unified working class. What is preventing the creation of such a unified class today? Many things, but the number one reason historically has been white supremacy and the system of privileges that capital grants to white workers in exchange for their loyalty to the system. (A side note: contrary to Mike E.'s claims, I absolutely include the white middle class in this devil's bargain. What is the 20th century middle class but, by and large, those persons whose parents or grandparents escaped from the working class, usually through the system of racial preferences?) What must be done to break up this deal between capital and one section of the working class? The destruction of the white race, or if you prefer, the destruction of white supremacy and its system of petty privileges. Figuring out specific programs and campaigns to do this would constitute a dual power strategy in the United States. As revolutionaries, that is the task that faces us.

When it comes to building a dual power, the size of the organization or the numbers of people participating in a campaign doesn't matter; it's the potential that matters. If our strategy is sound, the numbers will follow. (This is why building a movement of thousands isn't inherently better than building a movement of dozens. What counts is what each movement is doing and how they are doing it.) Whatever the advantages the anti-cop working group had over the anti-austerity working group (and this might be its only advantage!), it was a working group that was proposed based on an analysis of the crucial role of whiteness in preventing the creation of a unified working class and it was defended on the basis that it represented a dual power strategy.

I'm not claiming that a dual power strategy will solve all problems and end all debates. Quite the contrary: there will be all sorts of discussion, disagreements, mistakes, and blunders. When is a strategy a dual power strategy? Does this particular project have dual power potential or not? Whose analysis of history is correct? There are also situations in which we will need to engage in work that can't build a dual power, such as solidarity work. But what a revolutionary group needs to do is to ask the right kinds of questions, and to do that we need the right kind of orientation. The "mass line" and "just equals" orientations ask the wrong questions, so their answers are inevitably wrong, too.

Conclusion

Regardless, Love and Rage is gone. In their anger, both camps have mostly been talking over each other. The WWB side is right to point out that the accusation that most of them aren't activists is a poor substitute for a real political critique. At the same time, they engage in the same sort of sniping by class baiting the anti-WWBers, calling them the "NYC student crew," etc.

You can't build a political organization without politics. The only thing that can help us anarchist or anti-authoritarian revolutionaries is a shared set of political principles and a willingness to put these principles in practice through propaganda, activism, error, and self-criticism. Unfortunately, neither side has set out a position on all three issues consistent with the one I have outlined here. To have any chance at building a free society, a revolutionary organization needs to struggle on all three fronts. One can have a situation of dual power without the counterpower being anti-authoritarian or even with it being white supremacist. (A slogan of the Rand Rebellion in 1921 in South Africa was "White workers of the world, unite!") Likewise, one can be against white supremacy and anti-authoritarian without working toward a dual power. I welcome proposals for forming a new organization based on the positions I've set out here and with a commitment to test out these positions in the streets.

5

After Winter Must Come Spring: a Self-Critical Evaluation of the Life and Death of the Love and Rage Revolutionary Anarchist Federation
BY THE FIRE BY NIGHT ORGANIZING COMMITTEE

ON MAY 23, 1998 THE LOVE AND RAGE Revolutionary Anarchist Federation dissolved. Several days later, after a series of meetings, a number of its former members launched the Fire by Night Organizing Committee. In this pamphlet, we try to evaluate our experiences with Love and Rage. We hope to draw lessons from our experience that will help us move forward in our continued struggle for social justice and freedom. The first part of this pamphlet relates to the history of Love and Rage: its origins, its course of development, and the events leading up to its final dissolution. The second part examines both the accomplishments and the failures of Love and Rage and looks for their roots in our theory and methods of work. The final section begins to address our vision of a reinvigorated revolutionary movement in the United States, and how we see Fire by Night contributing to its construction. Over the years, many Love and Rage members pointed out the weaknesses that are acknowledged here, but were not listened to. Some of them left the organization out of frustration. Others stuck it out to the end. Some of them are part of Fire by Night, while others are not. This pamphlet is dedicated to all of those people who struggled to make Love and Rage the organization it should have been, but never was.

PART I: A BRIEF HISTORY

Love and Rage was founded as a "continental revolutionary anarchist new monthly" with a section in Spanish, at a conference in Chicago in November 1989. The roughly seventy-five people who founded Love and Rage included several representatives of anarchist collectives from across the United States and Canada, a number of individual anarchist activists, and about twenty former members of the Revolutionary Socialist League (RSL), a small Trotskyist group that had turned towards anarchism in the late 1980s. The prospects for building a revolutionary anarchist organization in North America looked particularly bright. During the 1980s, a vibrant anarchist movement composed mainly of small collectives and affinity groups had sprouted and established itself as a radical and militant voice within a number of larger social movements. From nuclear disarmament to South African and Central American solidarity to ACT UP to campus organizing, anarchists played an important role, pushing for democracy in these movements and for direct action in the streets. At the same time, the traditional Marxist left was in a state of advanced decomposition. The Tiananmen Square massacre, the collapse of the Soviet empire, and the electoral defeat of the Sandinistas all suggested the irrelevance of the old Marxist left and the importance of anti-authoritarianism to any revived movement. Increased activity in the social movements suggested space for a new force—a serious and dedicated revolutionary anarchist organization—that could consolidate the scattered anarchist groups and individuals to deepen their impact on the tone and character of this upsurge. Love and Rage was the only revolutionary organization of national scope founded in this period whose creators didn't come out of the upsurge of the 1960s and

1970s. With the exception of the ex-RSL members, we had little or no experience trying to build a serious revolutionary organization. Despite this fact (or because of it), we were very optimistic about our new project. This optimism allowed us to accomplish things that many predicted we wouldn't, but it also led to a number of the mistakes that would ultimately spell the demise of Love and Rage eight years later.

FROM NEWSPAPER TO NETWORK

From the beginning, most people involved in Love and Rage saw the newspaper as a vehicle to build a continental organization, or at least a firmer infrastructure for a revolutionary anarchist movement. By building the structure necessary to write, produce and distribute a genuinely continental newspaper, we were putting in place the basic elements of an organization. We used the newspaper to build anarchist participation in the Earth Day 20th anniversary actions being organized by the Left Greens and the Youth Greens in the spring of 1990. During the Gulf War, Love and Rage issued a call for an anarchist contingent to a March on Washington that broke away from the main demonstration and carried out an attack on World Bank headquarters. The Gulf War marked an important turning point for radical politics in the US. While opposition to the war was massive, it proved unable to put a brake on the wholesale slaughter of at least 100,000 Iraqis by US-led forces or even register much on American national consciousness. Ironically, the lull in activity following the war contributed to the growth of Love and Rage as many smaller anarchist projects fell apart and their members looked for something to grab onto. After a year and a half of monthly publication and intense participation in the Earth Day and Gulf War work, supporters of the newspaper held our second conference in the summer of 1991 in Minneapolis, Minnesota. There we formally constituted ourselves as the Love and Rage Network. The Network took on two ill-fated organizing projects for 1992 that led to crisis a year down the line. One campaign advocated a boycott of the 1992 presidential elections. The other, an Anti-Racist Summer Project, targeted a working-class white neighborhood in East St. Paul, Minnesota where nazi skinheads and the KKK were actively organizing. The boycott campaign fizzled because Love and Rage was unable to build a strong and broad enough coalition. The Anti-Racist Summer Project, organized in conjunction with Twin Cities Anti-Racist Action (ARA), relocated activists from across the US and Canada to East St. Paul for the summer to work full time building a community-based anti-racist bulkhead there. But the plan of action was unclear and more time was spent wrangling with internal dynamics than in any sort of effective organizing against the white supremacists.

FROM NETWORK TO ORGANIZATION

The failure of both our projects in 1992 brought on a crisis and some soul-searching. Two main perspectives emerged. One held that Love and Rage was too centralized and concentrated too much of its energy on building an organizational structure at the expense of building up strong local collectives. The opposing perspective stressed the maintenance and strengthening of a continental organization, united around a common politics and committed to developing and carrying out a common strategy. Folks in this camp proposed that we define membership in the organization, draft a set of bylaws, write a political statement, and concentrate our work in two or three key areas.

This conflict came to a head at Love and Rage's 1993 conference in San Diego. The organization-minded camp won out and we changed our name to the Love and Rage Revolutionary Anarchist Federation.

AMOR Y RABIA

In 1992, our Mexican comrades established a local in Mexico City. They began publishing a Spanish-language edition of the newspaper, *Amor y Rabia*, a year later. With this development, the US-based newspaper eliminated its Spanish section and started distributing the Mexican *Amor y Rabia* to our Spanish-language readership. The Mexican and US/Canadian sections of the organization began working more closely together after the Zapatista National Liberation Army (EZLN) launched their uprising on January 1, 1994 in the state of Chiapas. We promptly recognized that the politics of the EZLN were distinct from those of previous national liberation movements in ways that were important to anti-authoritarians. *Amor y Rabia* and *Love and Rage* became important early sources of information about the Zapatistas. We sought to provide direct material aid to the Zapatistas in a variety of forms. The most significant was the creation of the Martyrs of Chicago Direct Solidarity Encampment sponsored by Amor y Rabia for fourteen months in the Zapatista community of Santa Rosa El Copal. The Martyrs of Chicago Encampment brought forth a number of internal contradictions in Amor y Rabia that ultimately led to its disintegration as an organization.

THE SEARCH FOR A STRATEGY

From the beginning, Love and Rage lacked unity on any sort of overarching strategy for anarchist revolution in North America. Instead we had what was sometimes called "a strategy for a strategy." Since we didn't have the critical mass of people or experience to really articulate a coherent strategy, the argument went, we should instead work on getting enough anarchist activists together around certain elementary points of unity and areas of activity so that the discussion of strategy could really begin. This may have worked had the momentum of 1989 held out. But a revolutionary organization cannot be built on the basis of waiting for objective conditions to propel things forward. It must have a plan of action, no matter how modest. The most important step we took towards developing a strategy was to set up working groups. Working groups were meant to concentrate our activism in two or three areas so that we might have a greater impact. In practice, our selection of areas of work only ratified the choices members had already made as individuals. In the summer of 1995, the New York City local made a collective decision to concentrate our organizing work in the student movement at the City University of New York. Love and Rage members had played leadership roles in the movement against tuition hikes and budget cuts that spring, which had culminated in a demonstration of about 25,000 mostly Black and Latino young people, and many of them high school students. The CUNY student movement was our most successful break with the mainly-white anarchist scene and it gave us a much fuller understanding of how white skin privilege works to divide white radicals from the struggles of people of color. The members involved often found themselves challenged politically by the radical activists of color who were their closest comrades in the student movement. Questions came up that were difficult for anarchists to answer. For example, Love and Rage members had argued against getting a police permit for a march on Wall Street on March 23, 1995. Although students fought back bravely and militantly against the police, they had not been seasoned by years of radical street actions as most anarchists had been. 3,000 police prevented the march of 25,000 college and high school students from leaving City Hall by brutally beating, macing, and arresting students, many of whom were at their first demonstration. The student movement found itself unable to draw significant numbers to any event for years afterward. It became clearer to most activist members of the New York Love and Rage local that we needed to develop a strategy, one that would not rely on radical tactics alone, one that we could plan out and test in practice collectively.

THE DEBATE

The debates that led to the dissolution of Love and Rage have echoes going back to the founding of the organization. But the last chapter in the conflict began essentially with the publication of an essay called "The Historical Failure of Anarchism." The paper argued that the anarchist movement had failed to adequately confront its historical defeats, particularly in the Spanish Revolution, and so anarchism had become theoretically impoverished. It called on anarchists to re-examine certain assumptions and tenets, and to look at the experiences of non-anarchist revolutions in the 20th century for both positive and negative lessons. Most provocatively, it argued that the exclusive reliance on militias by anarchists in Spain had been a military disaster, and upheld the position of the Friends of Durruti who had called for the formation of a revolutionary army. While this essay was not intended as an attempt to outline a strategic orientation for Love and Rage, it quickly became the object of heated polemics that overshadowed the efforts to talk about a strategy for the organization. Two former members of the RSL wrote attacks on the essay that suggested that it was the first step down the slippery slope towards Stalinism. Many other members took issue with the essay as well. At this point, several members of the New York local sought to redirect the debate towards questions of organizing method, drawing variously on Paolo Friere's theories of pedagogy, Mao Ze Dong's theory of "mass line," and the Zapatistas' notion of "mandar obedeciendo" (leading by obeying). These members saw reflection on our own organizing as a necessary component of developing an effective revolutionary strategy. The ex-RSL members and several others attacked this organizing approach promoted by the New York members as reformist, and as a tailing after the lowest common denominator politics of the masses. Several ex-RSLers argued instead for the development of an "Anarchist Transitional Program" (presumably similar to the Transitional Program of the Trotskyists). This would be a program of demands, such as calling for a general strike, that anarchists should fight for in the course of reform struggles and would supposedly lead those struggles towards revolutionary conclusions. The debate over organizing method exposed how little anarchist theory has to say on the question. The main theoretical concepts on both sides of this debate were taken from outside anarchism, though some tried to dress them up with examples from anarchist history or calls to "read Malatesta."

THE BREAKUP

While many members of Love and Rage agreed and disagreed with both sides on various debates, two distinct camps eventually emerged. Those caught in the middle never coalesced into a distinct tendency of their own and found themselves forced to either choose sides or watch from the sidelines. In the Fall of 1997, thirteen members signed a factional document called "What We Believe," written by several ex-RSL members, which drew final lines in the debate. WWB laid out a list of principles it argued had been questioned by the writings or actions of other unnamed members. Much of WWB reiterated basic tenets of anarchism, which were generally accepted by everyone in Love and Rage. However, on some key points WWB was quite contentious. The first was a statement that all of the theoretical weaknesses of anarchism could be answered from "within anarchism." This singled out for attack those members who wanted Love and Rage to develop new living theory with influences from Marxism, feminism, revolutionary nationalism and elsewhere. The second point of debate centered on the question of the system of white skin privileges. WWB stated that white workers have only "petty and apparent" privileges over workers of color. It dismissed the idea that whites get very real material benefits from the racist system we live under, benefits which have blocked their effective participation in revolutionary struggles. Finally, WWB called for building democratic mass movements even though many of the signatories had not been involved in any mass work whatsoever for years. WWB forced everybody in Love and Rage to take sides by proclaiming that anybody who did not accept the document's principles had no place in the organization. Many members of the organization felt either that the document did not address issues crucial to Love and Rage's progress or that it was trying to force us to take a fighting stance on positions before we had had a thorough debate. WWB appeared when the organization was in a profound crisis, and it deepened that crisis. The Minneapolis local had ceased to function after three key members relocated to other cities. The New York local was paralyzed by the debates that had been taking place in the organization and stopped meeting after the summer of 1997. The Michigan-based coordinating committee elected at the March 1997 conference never met, with the result that no decisions could be made on the Federation level. Finally, a Federation conference was scheduled for May 1998 despite the complete non-functioning of all decision-making bodies. It was clear by this time that the organization was going to split. The only question was how ugly it would get and if anything was going to come out of it. Love and Rage's last conference took place on May 23, 1998 at Hunter College in New York City. The conference was mercifully brief and largely civil. The folks assembled presented their various projects and voted to dissolve the organization. Civility broke down only when we discussed a division of the resources. It became clear that the debts of the organization were greater than any resources and that the WWB faction had no intention of paying their share. Before the conference degenerated any further it was adjourned. Following the conference, a number of non-WWBers met in the Love and Rage office and founded the Fire by Night Organizing Committee.

PART 2: ACCOMPLISHMENTS AND MISTAKES
OUR ACCOMPLISHMENTS

The breakup of Love and Rage was demoralizing for many members. It is therefore important to make a critical analysis that acknowledges the real successes of the organization. Love and Rage was probably the most significant explicitly revolutionary anarchist organization in the United States in the latter half of the 20th century in terms of participation in mass struggles and in its influence on discussions within the anarchist movement and the broader left. Love and Rage was for the most part an organization of activists who participated in broader struggles. We played an important role in building a militant and anti-authoritarian wing within the movement against the US war in the Persian Gulf. We consistently promoted the causes of political prisoners in the pages of the newspaper and our members did important work for prison solidarity in general, and in the defense of the life of Mumia Abu-Jamal in particular. Love and Rage played important roles in the fight against Operation Rescue, in building Anti-Racist Action (ARA), in building solidarity with the Zapatistas, in the struggle against cutbacks, and in defense of open admissions at CUNY, in local struggles for welfare rights and for a living wage. In our work building Anti-Racist Action, Love and Rage members were committed to breaking out of the confines of the white male-dominated punk scene the movement started from. In Minneapolis, Love and Rage activists helped build an ARA group led by young women, and in Detroit, they helped build an ARA group that was mostly people of color. The most significant single accomplishment of Love and Rage was probably the continuous publication of the English and Spanish-language newspapers, which were the most reliably published anarchist periodicals in the US and Mexico in the 1990s. They were a source of international news that was otherwise largely unavailable in North America. For overseas readers, they were a consistent source of news about social struggles in the US and Mexico. The newspaper never simply rehashed a "line," but published articles from a variety of anti-authoritarian perspectives. We also published criticisms about ourselves even if we thought they lacked merit, and refused to publish attacks on other anarchist projects even when this policy was not reciprocated. As a result, Love and Rage was a very non-sectarian newspaper despite the controversies that continued to circle around the organization. Love and Rage fought for the development of a critical anti-authoritarian analysis of white supremacy rooted in the particular historical experience of North American society. We also struggled against the then-dominant position within the anarchist movement that crudely equated all nationalisms, whether imperialist forms of nationalism or anti-imperialist national liberation struggles. Love and Rage covered the struggles for reproductive freedom, against sexual violence, for a just response to the AIDS epidemic, and for queer liberation. We promoted the development of a radical movement for women's self-defense and empowerment. We sought to focus attention on the struggles of poor and working-class women and women of color. Over the years, we helped carve out significantly larger space for these politics within the anarchist movement. This space was filled by new groups and projects, many of whom had little awareness of how recently these politics had been treated with complete hostility within the anarchist movement. Love and Rage developed an internal structure and a set of processes for debate and discussion that were a dramatic improvement on the practices of the larger anarchist movement. Love and

Rage used a "modified consensus" method of decision-making that sought consensus but used majority votes to settle unresolvable issues. We tried to incorporate elements of feminist process developed by the women's liberation movement into our decision-making process as well. While these processes functioned imperfectly, they moved us toward a real democratic internal life as an organization.

OUR MISTAKES

Along the way, Love and Rage made some real if modest contributions to the development of revolutionary theory and practice in a very difficult period. But the fact remains that we failed to build the kind of organization we were convinced was necessary to bring about the kind of revolutionary change we still see as a condition for real human freedom. It is tempting to blame this failure on the times, or to blame it on this individual or that group of people within the organization. But revolutionary organizations must be able to survive hard times and to deal with the inevitable limitations of the people who make them up. The failure to meet such challenges is fundamentally a political failure which must have its roots in the theory and practice of the organization.

STEP-BY-STEP

One mistake made by some of the founders of Love and Rage was to think that people would, in a step-by-step fashion, come to see the necessity of the various component parts of a serious revolutionary organization. Some of the original proponents of the newspaper wanted to build a tighter organization from the start. Although they knew that others disagreed with them, they thought that people could struggle through differences over the ultimate vision as we went along, instead of splitting to work on separate projects. The main reason behind this error was that the anarchist tradition in which we placed ourselves had little historical experience and practically no serious theory for building the kind of organization we were trying to build. Some of our most basic ideas about our own project can be found in the Leninist tradition of which we were (and still are) critical. Many of these ideas are common sense features of any serious revolutionary organization: basic security precautions, the need for unity in theory and action, and a developed analysis of imperialism. Rather than honestly acknowledge a debt to Leninism, these members sought to restate the case for each of these elements within an anarchist framework and in reference to the historical experiences of the anarchist movement. We were convinced that we could redefine anarchism in a step-by-step manner as the success of each step pointed to the necessity of the next. The step-by-step approach worked to a degree. The newspaper became the basis for the Network, which led to the Federation. But many people were recruited to Love and Rage on the basis of what it was, because we weren't clear enough about what we wanted it to become. Some of these people would be won to the need for the next step, whatever that happened to be, but others tended to oppose it. The process of putting in place the most elementary features of an organization became agonizingly slow and many good people left over the years out of frustration with this glacial pace.

The RSL

From our inception, we deliberately played down the role of the ex-RSLers in Love and Rage. This was a response to the rabid sectarianism of much of the anarchist movement at that time, which led to a wholly distorted account of Love and Rage, portraying it as a creation of, or even a continuation of the RSL. In fact, of the twenty ex-RSLers who started out in Love and Rage, half were gone within a year. Most of the others either became completely inactive or else were barely active in the organization. This was probably linked to the demoralizing experience of dissolving the organization they had spent two decades building. There were several issues, in particular, the question of white skin privilege, on which most of the ex-RSLers were at odds with the majority position in the organization. They were able to carve out a certain space for their politics, even if they were not putting them into practice through mass work. In this way, they defined a range of debate and a number of "agreements to disagree" that made it harder for the organization to more precisely define its politics. The biggest impact the ex-RSLers made on the politics of Love and Rage was by what they did not do. The ex-RSLers had been part of a common organizational project rooted in the traditions of Marxism, Leninism, and Trotskyism for two decades, and yet they never made any attempt at a collective critical summation of that experience for the benefit of Love and Rage. This failure contributed to one of the biggest weaknesses in the political culture of Love and Rage, our repeated failure to sum up our experiences and try to draw lessons from them.

The "*Iskra* Principle"

Lenin used the newspaper *Iskra* (*The Spark*) to build a clandestine network of writers, editors, and distributors that became the skeleton of the Bolshevik Party in Russia at the turn of the century. Love and Rage was conceived along very similar lines. Ricardo Flores Magón did the same thing with *Regeneracion* and Malcolm X did it with *Muhammad Speaks*, but the truth is that the most coherent argument for this strategy was Lenin's. It was those arguments that had convinced some of us and that we used to convince others. There are important things to be learned from reading Lenin. The importance of having a newspaper is not one of them. Leaving aside the fairly obvious point that a clandestinely-circulated revolutionary newspaper is going to have more of an impact in pre-radio, turn-of-the-century, Czarist Russia than in the electronic-media saturated, late 20th century, United States of America, this reliance on a newspaper created big problems. The Bolsheviks' single-minded reliance on their press reflected their elitist self-conception as an organization of middle-class intellectual leaders bringing socialist consciousness to the working class. The central place of the newspaper is thus part of what's wrong with Lenin's idea of a vanguard party. Organizations built around newspapers tend to be defined less by the practice of their members in actual struggles and more by their line on various questions, a line that springs mainly from the heads of the leadership of the organization rather than from a process of reflection on the struggle as it is actually taking place. This is why the hard-working activists who build up the mass movements despise the groups that place such an emphasis on pushing their newspapers. Love and Rage members shared this contempt for the newspaper pushers and we never really fell into that pattern.

Although *Love and Rage* was not a line newspaper, the central place of the newspaper in the life of Love and Rage had a significant impact. For one, it impeded the development of a common strategic orientation because trying to come to some sort of strategy would inevitably chase off some of the support upon which the broadly-defined newspaper depended. Also, an organization built around a newspaper will tend to attract more aspiring writers and fewer natural organizers, a dynamic which did not help counter our organizational weaknesses.

WHITE CHAUVINISM

Love and Rage failed to consistently place the struggle against white supremacy at the center of our politics and to confront the inherent contradictions of being such a white organization. Love and Rage always had a few Black or Latino members in the US, but these members rarely played a leadership role in the organization. In terms of its public appearance in the United States and Canada, Love and Rage was for all intents and purposes a white organization. This reflected where we came from. The anarchist movement in the US is overwhelmingly white and closely associated with an overwhelmingly white counter-culture. While Love and Rage members engaged in a great deal of anti-racist work, we tended to treat racism as just one of a number of "issues" that members could choose to work on, rather than the strategically central question confronting revolutionaries in the United States. We thought of our work choices in a moralistic way instead of a strategic way. The purpose of a strategic focus would be to choose a particular struggle based on historical study of which communities have been able to mobilize the most powerful and most seminal movements in US history, not on who deserves to be liberated first. But we were unable to focus strategically and make the best use of our small numbers. Thus, when members worked in movements around poverty, women's liberation, and queer liberation, we often did so without a clear strategic conception of how to deal with the question of white supremacy in those areas of work. The questions of our politics on white supremacy and the racial composition of the organization cannot be tidily separated. From the beginning, most— if not all —of us rejected the model of a "white solidarity organization" merely supporting the struggles of people of color. In contrast to this model, we were committed to building a genuinely multi-racial revolutionary anarchist organization. The problem was that without a clear analysis of the nature of white supremacy, the workings of white skin privilege, and an organizational strategy for fighting them, the efforts of individual members to build such an organization were often at cross purposes. This problem always bubbled beneath the surface, but it finally erupted around two issues. The first was the decision of individuals to use the newspaper as a forum for heated polemics with Black nationalists. One white member of Love and Rage adopted the posture of a member of the Black community in these arguments. This was dishonest, opportunist and racist, but we had no clear policy to prevent or discipline such practices. The second incident involved the publication of an editorial declaring our commitment to becoming a multi-racial organization. The editorial was an attempt at a compromise after two earlier editorials were rejected for their white chauvinism. We should never have tried to compromise on such issues. This in itself reflected our white chauvinism. Publicly declaring our commitment to becoming a genuinely multi-racial organization without having clarified in advance our analysis of white supremacy and our program for combating it only created the impression that we wanted to darken our ranks to make ourselves feel good, even if this was not the actual attitude of most of the organization. White chauvinism in Love and Rage also took the form of white guilt. We were at various times criticized by people of color both for our failure to systematically reach out to Black folks and for having a colonialist attitude in our efforts to do so. Rather than grapple with the difficult issues involved, we tended to either accept these criticisms in their totality or to not respond to them. In this way, we not only gave credence to criticisms that were entirely baseless, we undermined our own ability to deal with the valid criticisms of our practice. In effect, we put our personal desires to be validated by people of color ahead of our commitment to understand and fight white supremacy.

US Chauvinism

A related problem in Love and Rage was US chauvinism. The root of this problem was our pretensions to being a continental organization. Love and Rage was always dominated by the US section of the organization. Our treatment of Canadian reality tended to be tokenistic, and reflected the widespread national chauvinist sentiment in the US (even among radicals and revolutionaries) that Canada is "just the 51st state." The Canadian section of Love and Rage remained quite small, so there was never much pressure to really face these contradictions. The relations between the US and Mexican sections proved more problematic precisely because our Mexican section, Amor y Rabia, became a significant force within Mexico's small anarchist movement. Love and Rage never formally acknowledged the existence of distinct national sections. In effect, we had separate organizations pretending to be one. The relationship of the US section to the Mexican section was largely one of solidarity, in the form of financial support for the publication of *Amor y Rabia* and various other activities of the Mexican section. In the end, we were effectively subsidizing the sectarian and authoritarian antics of a couple of leaders of the Mexican section (who had the most direct contacts with the US organization). That only served to discredit the larger organization. Put bluntly, having a Mexican section raised the standing of Love and Rage in the US, and in order to preserve this relationship we turned a blind eye to abuses we should have seen. This was only a disservice to our Mexican comrades, since it perpetuated problems in their organization. It was national chauvinism and opportunism on our part.

Sexism

Love and Rage had some very strong and intelligent women. Still, men outnumbered women by nearly two to one and took up even more time in meetings than was proportional to their numbers. We tried to counter sexist dynamics by putting women in positions of leadership (although we did this sporadically) and by using feminist group process and facilitation. We had a sort of informal mentoring system for younger and newer women members who would be taken under the wing of a more experienced woman who would share her skills and help the newer member to make a place for herself in the organization. In the end, the individual and informal strategies we relied on were not enough to successfully combat the deeply entrenched male domination in Love and Rage. Aside from our inconsistent work in the struggle for reproductive freedom, and welfare organizing done by one or two members, Love and

Rage never did any other explicitly feminist long-term work. As individual women and men, most of us struggled with men in the activist groups we worked in over their sexism and promoted women's leadership in those groups. We usually had one working group that we attempted to give a "feminist lens," but the success or failure of this integration of feminism into our other work was usually determined by the willingness of individual women to repeatedly push for the small measures it would entail even after the larger vision of it had been passed by a vote at the conference. Women in Love and Rage reached a point of collectively coming together to criticize sexist dynamics in Love and Rage after some particularly glaring incidents. At one conference we held a meeting with a representative from BACORR, a radical reproductive freedom group in the Bay Area, about starting a national campaign that would struggle around issues of sterilization abuse and other related issues that affected primarily women of color and poor women, as well as clinic defense. No men from Love and Rage showed up at the meeting, although the ideas we were discussing addressed some of the men's criticisms that the clinic-defense focus of the feminist work we were doing only appealed to middle-class white women. Because the men weren't doing any explicitly feminist work, and we never developed an internal political education program, they never had to educate themselves about women's experiences of oppression and the history of women's resistance. Even after one woman put together a set of readings on revolutionary feminism, and each local had agreed to start a study group using it, only the New York local ever began a study group. Our problems of organizational liberalism and lack of discipline led to an inability to get the organization as a whole to take up feminist questions in our theory and practice.

ORGANIZATIONAL LIBERALISM

Many of the problems Love and Rage had can be connected to the general problem of organizational liberalism. We had a spirit of tolerance for practices that revolutionary organizations cannot afford to put up with. It took us nearly four years to establish any expectations of membership. After that, we progressively tightened up those expectations on paper, but since we never provided for any enforcement mechanism the expectations were meaningless. Many took advantage of the "do your own thing" atmosphere, dropping in and out of activity, in some cases for years at a stretch. "Members" who never met the expectations of membership were frequently outspoken in their opposition to any attempt to further raise the expectations. Despite the fact that the dues structure was designed precisely to make sure those with the most money paid the highest rates, opposition to making it mandatory was framed in terms of not imposing it on the poorest members. As a result, a minority of members from all income brackets carried the weight of the organization while the majority paid their dues only when and if they felt like it. Organizational liberalism also contributed to a culture which effectively discouraged the sort of serious political debate that was a prerequisite for hammering out a political statement or strategy. Instead, there was a constant effort to deal with contradictions in the organization by finding compromise or consensus positions, even if those positions provided no real guidance for the organization. There was a consistent refusal to criticize ourselves or each other. Often, problems were only dealt with after they had gotten out of control. When members took on tasks for the organization, there was no effective mechanism to ensure that they were carried out. When the failure to carry out tasks was pointed out, this criticism was generally met with excuses rather than a serious evaluation of the problem. This common problem reached its most absurd proportions when the Michigan-based coordinating committee—the day-to-day decision-making body of the Federation between annual conferences—failed to meet once in the last year, while its members engaged in factional activity.

NO LEADERSHIP DEVELOPMENT

Anarchism tends to assume a theoretical posture of total hostility towards leadership. But every anarchist group or project that lasts any length of time has clearly identifi-able, if informal, leadership. Some groups deny what is obvious to outside observers. Others grudgingly concede the truth, but only to say they are fighting against the problem. Love and Rage did both. The fact of leadership in organizations and move-ments creates problems. A position of leadership is in some sense unavoidably a posi-tion of authority. As anti-authoritarians, we need to create systems that make leaders accountable to the broader body of people who make up a movement or organization. We must also develop a practice of leadership that consciously subverts those author-itarian tendencies, and assists in generalizing leadership skills among the people. The structure of Love and Rage did not allow for the fact that the organization had lead-ers. Our structure was exquisitely democratic in providing for the fullest participation by everybody in the decisions of the organization. The coordinating committee, with responsibility for day-to-day decision-making, was conceived of mainly as an admin-istrative body with no power to chart the course of the organization. The federation council was composed of delegates elected by locals who were expected to simply transmit the decisions of the membership. The result was a cumbersome process that was consistently unable to make decisions on time. Demonstrations and projects like speaking tours were finally endorsed a month or two after they were over! By failing to delegate real leadership responsibilities to these bodies, we only reinforced the power of the informal and therefore unaccountable leadership of the organization—the people who took things into their own hands to make sure the work kept getting done. Our failure to confront the issue of leadership meant that we were never able to solve these problems. The generally accepted notion of our relationship to mass movements was that we would simply participate in them as equals, arguing for our politics but not seeking leadership. (A more sophisticated version of this conception is the notion of the "leadership of ideas" promoted by the tendency in anarchism known as the Platformists, after "The Platform of the Libertarian Communists.") This concept, while appealing, swept under the rug the real contradictions in our actual relationships with mass movements. Many members of Love and Rage played leader-ship roles, whether they were willing to acknowledge them or not, in building various mass organizations and coalitions including Anti-Racist Action, the Vermont Living Wage Campaign, and the Student Liberation Action Movement (SLAM!) at CUNY. In all of these formations we fought for the maximum level of internal democracy and against a dependence on leaders. But as experienced activists with accumulated skills, access to resources, and an overarching social analysis, we consistently found ourselves fulfilling leadership functions in these movements. The insistence that all activists in these movements participated as equals contradicted reality. It also protected us from being held responsible for mistakes that we committed as leaders, and undermined any systematic development of leadership skills among new people. It is clear to us now that there can be no social revolution without some sort of organized revolutionary leadership. We still recognize that leadership has inherent authoritarian tendencies which tend to reproduce the oppressive structures of this society and which must be fought. We are opposed to any conception of leadership that grants special privileges to leaders. We believe that one of the primary functions of a revolutionary organization must be the development of effective, responsible, and accountable leadership. This means, in addition to our insistence on movement democracy, the ongoing and systematic political education and organizational skills training of its members, as well as the promotion of these same processes as broadly as possible within the mass movements.

LACK OF METHOD

In the course of the debate that destroyed Love and Rage, two philosophies on the question of organizational method emerged. While both sides sought to emphasize the supposedly anti-authoritarian character of their theories, both drew on the works of decidedly authoritarian tendencies in Marxism. Several of the people who went on to found Fire by Night argued for what they described as the Zapatista theory of mandar obedeciendo or "leading by obeying," which shares much in common with Paolo Friere's ideas on pedagogy and the Maoist theory of the mass line. It attempts to address the inherent contradiction between the fact of leadership and the goal of the self-organization of the people. The basic principle is that the people learn by doing, and that the germ of revolutionary consciousness exists and finds constant expression in the experiences of the oppressed in struggle. This germ exists alongside all sorts of other ideas, including many reactionary ones. Revolutionaries should, in struggle with the people, draw out the revolutionary content in how they already understand their conditions, clarify it, and distinguish it from the reactionary ideas. Through the constant repetition of this process, a more fully developed revolutionary consciousness emerges that is the organic product of people's experiences in struggle. In contrast to this approach, several signers of WWB advocated the development of an Anarchist Transitional Program, as mentioned earlier. The advocates of a Transitional Program sought to depict the method of mandar obedeciendo as one of simply following the masses and upholding whatever they believed, in order to manipulate and gain leadership over the movement. The advocates of mandar obedeciendo argued that the idea of a tiny group developing a program that would supposedly become the revolutionary program of the masses, without the participation of the masses themselves in this process, was inherently vanguardist. From cradle to grave, these contradictory conceptions of organizing method coexisted in Love and Rage, so that we never overcame our confusion about what kind of organization we had. At times, Love and Rage followed the Trotskyist practice of re-writing the *New York Times* coverage of international news and then plugging in our instant anarchist analysis. At other times, we used the paper to draw out the lessons we were learning through our participation in various struggles. The lack of clarity about organizational method also led to a lack of clarity about the distinction between a mass organization and a revolutionary organization. Our attempts to develop new theory from the lessons of our mass work were not always rigorous. This further blurred the distinction as members of the organization rightly asked what Love and Rage had to offer that they weren't getting in their mass work.

THEORETICAL AND PRACTICAL WEAKNESSES OF ANARCHISM

The debates that destroyed Love and Rage began with a critique of the failure of anarchism to draw the right lessons from its historical defeats and failures. They ended with a number of people in the organization doubting the viability of anarchism as a theoretical framework for revolutionary politics in the 21st century, in some cases to the point of saying they were no longer anarchists. The final test of any system of ideas is the results it produces in practice. We hold Christianity responsible for the Crusades, the witch hunts, and the intolerance of contemporary fundamentalism. We hold Leninism responsible for mass starvation resulting from forced collectivization in the Soviet Union and China, as well as for the anti-democratic practices of various Leninist groups today. Similarly, anarchism must be judged by its results. Anarchism has had its brief moments as a serious revolutionary movement, but they have been few and have all gone down to defeat. Anarchism has been almost completely marginalized for over half a century and shows no real signs of emerging from its current semi-comatose condition. Revolutionary theory must be a living and vibrant body of ideas in constant contact with the actual struggles of oppressed people. Despite the best efforts of ourselves and others, this does not describe contemporary anarchism. This is not to suggest that anarchism has nothing to offer. Many of us have identified as anarchists for many years, and our politics continue to owe a great deal to anarchism. We believe that the reproduction of the authoritarian relations of this society within our movements, and in a new society, is one of the primary dangers confronting the revolutionary project. We do not currently see any other existing body of theory and practice as adequately answering our questions. If we want to develop a revolutionary politics that can fight for and win real human liberation in the 21st century, we must ruthlessly attack the flaws in all existing revolutionary theory and search for the ideas that can be used. Leaving aside the question of whether anarchism can be reconceived in a way that answers the questions that arose in these debates, we will identify the weaknesses of anarchist theory and practice that contributed to Love and Rage's downfall.

PHILOSOPHICAL IDEALISM

The first of these weaknesses is philosophical idealism, or the construction of a theory of society on a basis of abstract ideas rather than on the empirical investigation of material reality. This use of the term "idealism" should not be confused with the popular use of the word to speak of people who fight for an ideal of a better society. In this sense, we are proudly idealists. As anarchists, we defined ourselves as anti-statists —in other words, we viewed the state as inherently oppressive and as an instrument for the rule of a minority class. This is true, and can be supported with all sorts of evidence. But it does not help us figure out how to build directly democratic instruments of self-governance under conditions of social collapse, or to carry out the transition to a truly free society. In a revolutionary situation, the people will have to nationalize an economy, provide reparations to oppressed nations, repress counter-revolutionaries, equalize healthcare, coordinate an army, and figure out how to do all this efficiently without building a new oppressive state. What will we do with white neighborhoods like Bensonhurst, Brooklyn, which has traditionally greeted Black people who venture into the neighborhood with racist violence? Do we force them at gun-point to integrate, try using the mass line to struggle with them, or let them have autonomous self-determination? What we need is a theory of the state that starts with an empirical investigation of the origins of the state, the state as it actually exists today, the various experiences of revolutionary dual power, and post-revolutionary societies. We expect such a theory would confirm the anarchist hostility to the state as an instrument for human liberation, but we also expect that it would challenge the simplistic way that anarchists treat the question of the state. Why did pre-state societies consistently give birth to or find themselves conquered by state societies? Why does the state perform socially useful as well as repressive and exploitive functions? Are all states (monarchies, liberal democracy, one-party dictatorships) equal? Why have the brief modern experiences of revolutionary self-government (the Paris Commune, the Soviets and Workers Councils, the original Zapatistas in the Mexican Revolution, the Spanish Revolution) all gone down so quickly to defeat? These questions can only be answered after a serious investigation of historical experience. Love and Rage never systematically undertook that investigation, but instead fell back on the formulaic responses of anarchist orthodoxy.

MORALISM

Anarchism exists more as an ethical posture than a developed political theory. This is both a virtue and a vice. Anarchism's insistence on the ethical dimension of the society we are fighting for and the way we fight for it contrasts starkly with the repeated apologies for the repression of basic democratic rights, forced collectivization, and mass murder in the name of progress and "scientific" socialism. To acknowledge that the new society will inevitably bear some of the marks of the old, does not mean anything goes. The flip side of this is anarchism's persistent tendency to substitute a moral posture for a strategic political perspective. Ethical principles tend to offer better guidance on what not to do than on what to do. In Love and Rage, political positions were often judged not in terms of their validity, but on their appeal to righteousness. This led to an over-eager embrace of the most strident formulations and a tendency to shut down debate when issues got complicated. The persistent refusal of the anarchist movement as a whole to learn any serious lessons from its defeats suggests to us the deep-rootedness of these theoretical weaknesses.

PART 3: THE LEFT NEXT TIME

Capitalism has entered into a new period marked by a dramatic increase in the global integration of the economy, and an all-out war on the poor that has sought to roll back all of the gains of the various social movements of the past century. Resistance to the new world order breaks out every day, in every corner of the globe, and the potential for more resistance is immense. At the same time, the organized left has never been weaker. There is a crying need for a reinvigorated revolutionary left that is able to incorporate the lessons of the past century and respond creatively to the challenges of the next one. The left we need must be radically democratic, by which we mean there must be a break with the authoritarian and anti-democratic practices widely associated with Leninism. The left we need must be multi-racial, which means it must fully incorporate the insights and demands of the oppressed nationality movements, and must have leadership that is rooted in these movements. The left we need must be feminist. It must integrate an understanding of patriarchy as a historic and contemporary reality, and use the practices of feminist process developed by the women's movement. Women must be in real leadership positions, and not just tokens. The left we need must uphold queer liberation and must include gay, lesbian, bisexual and transgendered leadership. The left we need must be independent of the capitalist political parties and institutions, and based in the communities of oppressed people. The left we need must be a true expression of the self-organization of the oppressed. In a revolutionary situation, it must be able to make use of the intellectual skills of individuals trained in political theory or economic planning without giving up the people's collective power to these individuals and creating a new ruling class. The precedents for the kind of left we need are few. But across the US and around the world, we see glimmers of it. We take particular inspiration from the Zapatistas in Mexico and the emerging international movement against neoliberalism that their example and prodding has inspired. We recognize that the Zapatistas are a new force, and do not imagine that they have all the answers. However, they have been able to overcome many of the sectarian divisions of the old left and reconceive the revolutionary project on a radical democratic foundation. Under conditions of siege by the Mexican Army, the EZLN has carried out decisions directly made by every woman, child and man in the indigenous villages that support it. While consensus decision-making on such a broad scale may not work in large cites, we can learn from the Zapatistas how important it is for a revolutionary movement to earn the support of its communities every step that it takes. The Fire by Night Organizing Committee is a product of the historical experiences of Love and Rage. We see the failure of anarchism in general and of Love and Rage in particular as part of the general failure of the revolutionary left in the 20th century. We believe that anarchism and the broader libertarian socialist tradition offer crucial insights into the failure of the state socialist experiences that must be integrated into any genuinely liberatory revolutionary politics in the 21st century. While we believe that the old categories that have historically divided the left are increasingly obsolete, and we repudiate the sectarianism of all tendencies on the left, we do not believe that we can simply put history behind us and all agree to get along. The construction of a reinvigorated revolutionary left will require, among other things, grappling with the roots of the failures of every tendency on the left. It will require not just coming to agreement on a program, but also developing unity in practice through concrete common work.

OUR PROJECT

Fire by Night is a small organization committed to building an organized revolutionary left in the United States. We view our own organization as provisional, in the sense that we do not imagine that our small group is the nucleus of the organization we want to be a part of. In this sense, we regard all existing organizations on the left as provisional. None of them meet even the most basic criteria for the kind of organization that needs to be built. For our first year, we have taken on an intensive program of political study and training. To more fully understand the issues that destroyed Love and Rage, we have taken on detailed study sessions on the state, class structure, patriarchy and white supremacy. To research the historical failures of the revolutionary experiences of the 20th century, we are studying the Mexican Revolution, the

Russian Revolution, the Spanish Revolution, the Chinese Revolution, the decolonization of Africa, the Cuban Revolution and Latin America, and the US in the '60s and
'70s. With the aim of becoming more effective and well-rounded revolutionary organizers, we have planned topics on organizing method and organizational structure. We
have committed ourselves to continued work in mass struggles, with a special focus
on poor people's struggles and the student movement. Our local in the Bay Area
works to organize tenants in public housing, who are fighting the city's plans to
remove them to clear the way for gentrification. Our local in New York City continues
to work with their comrades in CUNY, now to organize high school students, as well
as their families and communities, to fight for access to public higher education. We
are looking for people who share our perspective who want to work with us. We also
want to develop relations with other revolutionary forces in the US— to talk, to clarify and struggle over differences, and to see what sort of basis exists for common work.
We believe that the creation of a vibrant revolutionary left in the United States will
require a ruthless self-criticism of our failures to date. We have sought to make such a
criticism of ourselves in these pages, and hope that our efforts in this direction will
serve an example to others.